A STR⏐
THAT CHANGES
THE DENOMINATION

Anglican Evangelicals, the Conversion of England
and the Transformation of the Anglican Church

John P Richardson

A STRATEGY THAT CHANGES THE DENOMINATION
Anglican Evangelicals, the Conversion of England
and the Transformation of the Anglican Church
by John P Richardson

Published by Lulu, Rayleigh N.C. 2011

ISBN 978-1-4478-5667-2

Bible quotations are from THE HOLY BIBLE, NEW INTERNATIONAL VERSION®, NIV® Copyright © 1973, 1978, 1984, 2011 by Biblica, Inc.™ Used by permission.

Cover design and photo © John Richardson

A Strategy the Changes the Denomination is produced in the UK by:

MPA Books
39, Oziers
Elsenham
Bishop's Stortford
HERTS
CM22 6LS

+44(0)1279 813703

E-mail enquiries to j.p.richardson@virgin.net

A Strategy that Changes the Denomination
is available online from www.lulu.com

Also to be available from Amazon.

Contents

Preface

In July of 2011, I and some friends organized what eventually became the Anglican Evangelical Junior Clergy Conference. The stated aim of the AEJCC was to identify and encourage a future generation of Anglican clergy leaders, beginning with those who were currently exploring ordination, in training, in a curacy or in their first incumbency. The initial motivation was simply a sense that people were looking for guidance and direction about their Anglican and evangelical identity. In the process of preparing for and participating in the Conference, however, a new perception began to emerge of how to address the problems confronting the Church.

Inspiration for this came from two documents. One was the 1945 Church of England report *Towards the Conversion of England*, a copy of which I happened to pick up at a local church fête several years ago. The other was a small book with a long title, *Reorienting a Church for Accelerated Growth: With Special Reference to the Anglican Diocese of Taita Taveta, Kenya*, by Bishop Samson Mwaluda, lent to me by a member of Crosslinks.

Together, these books have helped reshape my own thinking about what needs to happen in and for the Church of England. What unites them is a vision for evangelistic mission carried out not by sections of the Church but by the Church as a whole. And as our own conference went forward it became clear that this provided a challenging vision for ourselves as Anglican evangelicals.

The Anglican evangelical constituency has, for over a hundred years, had an uneasy relationship with its parent body. In recent decades that has been compounded by a resurgence of divisions amongst evangelicals themselves.

The first section of this booklet catalogues the post-war period. It is written from an avowedly 'conservative evangelical' position. Nevertheless, I have tried to be even-handed in my criticisms throughout, since it is my firm conviction that evangelicals of every type have made serious mistakes. Common to all, however, has been a general acceptance that on the one hand there are 'evangelicals' and on the other there is 'the Church of England', and that whatever else happened, the two would (and probably should) always remain distinct.

The inevitable outcome, naturally, is that the mission of evangelicals and the mission of the Church of England are seen as two different things — a viewpoint that is certainly part of the institutional ethos.

Evangelicals naturally want to evangelize, and the rest of the Church of England might want to evangelize too. Certainly it would not stand in the way of evangelicals doing evangelism in their own areas and parishes. But, it is supposed, the Church of England might also want to do other things — in fact 'other things' are generally exactly what it wants to do, and it pours resources into doing them. And those 'other things' are also seen as a legitimate focus for congregational life and parish ministry, even if evangelism is nowhere in evidence.

The problem is that evangelicals, for their part, have largely accepted this *status quo* — some grudgingly, regarding the Church of England as a lost cause, others happily, regarding the securing of their place within the institution as one of the great achievements of the last fifty years. Either way, evangelism understood 'evangelically' remains a minority pastime. Meanwhile this difference of attitude has given evangelicals yet another reason to fall out amongst themselves.

The conviction emerging from the AEJCC, however, was that it shouldn't, and needn't, be like this. On the contrary, the whole Church of England could and should be involved in the work of evangelism, seeking the conversion of the nation. That was the plan in 1945, and we ought to have no embarrassment in appealing now to what was proposed as a proper agenda for the Church of England then.

The contribution of Bishop Mwaluda's book was to demonstrate how developing an agenda for radical growth in an Anglican context really requires confronting institutional change at every level. It is not enough for individual clergy or congregations to rush enthusiastically into the breach left by denominational neglect. To address most effectively the spiritual needs of a city, a region or a nation requires effort from the whole Church operating throughout the institution, beginning (preferably) with the bishop and his staff.

Unfortunately, we are very far from having a situation in the Church of England where many bishops are prepared to act in this way. But we can, and must, begin from where we are. In the second part of the booklet, therefore, specific suggestions are put forward. This is not an exhaustive set of proposals. Rather, it is an illustration of the kind of things which need to be considered and includes several 'case studies', some of which illustrate success, others of which ended in relative failure. The hope, however, is that this will spark some initiatives amongst other evangelical Anglicans.

Above all, this booklet calls for a change of attitude. We cannot afford to be either cynical or self-congratulatory. Christ commissioned his Church to take the gospel to the nations. The Church of England therefore ought to have as a priority taking the gospel to the English nation. Yet that is not happening and evangelicals have not really addressed the issue.

The AEJCC did not produce a 'conference statement', and the contents of this booklet are ultimately entirely my own. Nevertheless, the booklet itself is also part of a process that began there — a process which I hope may ultimately lead to changes in our denomination that make it a more effective instrument for the conversion of England.

John P Richardson
October 2011

Part 1
The Proclamation of the Gospel: Anglican Evangelicalism and the Post-war Challenge

In June 1945, towards the end of the Second World War, the Church of England published a report titled *Towards the Conversion of England*, setting out in detail an ambitious programme to reach the nation with the gospel through a transformed and mission-focused national church.[1]

Following a resolution of the Church Assembly in 1943, the Archbishops of Canterbury and York had set up a commission instructed to report back with plans for "definite action" to meet the spiritual needs of "present-day men and women".[2] And thus, over the next two years, small groups met across the country under wartime conditions "to survey the whole problem of modern evangelism, with special reference to the spiritual needs and prevailing intellectual outlook of the non-worshipping members of the community".[3]

The report was the outcome of their efforts, and though some of the details might be open to criticism (nothing is ever perfect), and other parts seem inevitably dated, its express desire for "conversion" must surely be applauded by modern evangelicals, as would be the definition of evangelism set out in the very first paragraph:

> To evangelize is so to present Christ Jesus in the power of the Holy Spirit, that men shall come to put their trust in God through Him, to accept Him as their Saviour, and serve Him as their King in the fellowship of His Church.[4]

---

[1] Commission on Evangelism, *Towards the Conversion of England* (London: The Press and Publications Board of the Church Assembly, 1945). Though postwar rationing doubtless affected the size of print runs, it is noteworthy that the publication enjoyed no fewer than six reprints before the end of 1945. Extracts from *Towards the Conversion of England* may be found at the Ugley Vicar blog http://ugleyvicar.blogspot.com.

[2] *Ibid.* para 2.

[3] *Ibid.* vi, 'Terms of Reference'.

[4] *Ibid.* para 1, though see Jim Packer, *Evangelism and the Sovereignty of God* (Leicester: Inter-Varsity Press, 1976), pp 37-40, who argues that strictly the definition detracts from God's sovereignty by putting a consecutive clause ("that men *shall* come")

However, the report also recognized explicitly the need not just for the proclamation of the gospel to the nation, but the transformation of the Church by the same gospel in order for it to become an instrument of proclamation:

> We cannot expect to get far with evangelism until three facts are faced. First, the vast majority of English people need to be converted to Christianity. Secondly, a large number of Church people also require to be converted, in the sense of their possessing that personal knowledge of Christ which can be ours only by the dedication of the whole self, whatever the cost. Thirdly, such personal knowledge of Christ is the only satisfactory basis for testimony to others.
>
> *It will thus be realised that the really daunting feature of modern evangelism is not the masses of the population to be converted, but that most of the worshipping community are only half-converted.* The aim of evangelism must be to appeal to all, within as well as without the Church, for that decision for Christ which shall make the state of salvation we call conversion the usual experience of the normal Christian. [Emphasis added][5]

If any individual or group today feels that all is not well with the Church of England, they may rest assured this was officially recognized many years ago! Nor did the report pull any punches when specifying the nature of the problem:

> ... the Church is ill-equipped for its unparalleled task and opportunity. The laity complain of a lack of creative leadership among all ranks of the clergy. The spiritual resources of the worshipping community are at a low ebb. Above all, the Church has become confused and uncertain in the proclamation of its message, and its life has ceased to reflect clearly the truth of the Gospel. It is for the Church, in this day of God, by a rededication of itself to its Lord, to receive from Him that baptism of Holy Ghost and of fire which will empower it to sound the call and give the awaited lead.[6]

The fact that those words still seem appropriate in the twenty-first century is surely an indictment of the way the Church of England

---

where a final clause should be (that "they *may* come"). The danger is that evangelism is then defined by its humanly-achieved *results*.

[5] *Ibid.* para 81.

[6] *Ibid.* para 33.

spent the subsequent sixty-six years.

So what went wrong?

In October 1944, William Temple, the Archbishop of Canterbury who had inspired the commission and the report, died at Westgate-on-Sea in Kent. His replacement, Geoffrey Fisher, was a man of a very different temper, and what the Church of England actually did over the next two decades was to revise the Canons of 1604.

Although, as the date indicates, this revision was long overdue (and indeed had commenced before the war), a reviewer of a recent biography of Fisher is surely right in describing it as "a glaring example of mistaken priorities".[7]

When the revision of the Canons was completed, the next item on the Church's agenda was liturgical revision, which from the early sixties went on for the remainder of the century. And whilst that process was still going on, the Church was already immersing itself in the issues of women's ordination, and now consecration, which have dominated Synod debates and electoral campaigns.

Only in 1988 was there a belated nod in the direction of the 1945 agenda, with the declaration at the Lambeth Conference of a 'Decade of Evangelism'. Some have claimed this actually led to a significant shift in the Church's approach to mission, resulting in the emergence of the 'Fresh Expressions' movement. Arguably, however, the fact that the term *fresh* expressions of church was coined to describe these new initiatives was a tacit admission that *old* expressions of church — which remain the vast majority — had been by-passed. Yes, the gospel might be being proclaimed in new ways, but the Church was not transformed for evangelistic mission and the decade generally had little discernible impact.

Of course, had things gone differently after the war, then evangelical Anglicans might have found themselves playing a central rôle in the life of the Church, given their existing commitment to gospel proclamation and their testimony to the

---

[7] Donald Gray, review of *Geoffrey Fisher, Archbishop of Canterbury 1945-1961*, by David Hein, *The Journal of Ecclesiastical History*, (2008) 59, 801.

resultant transformation of life. As it was, they found themselves entering the post-war era as a minority within an organization whose outward style was predominantly Anglo-catholic yet whose underlying theology was increasingly liberal.

Nevertheless, evangelical Anglican ministry continued with commendable vigour. In the parishes, the Church Pastoral Aid Society provided a 'cradle to college' structure of youth activities via CYPECS groups (in descending age-order, CYFA, Pathfinders, Explorers and Climbers). CPAS also published a widely-used 'family service', which in many parishes formed the backbone of Sunday morning gatherings.

In the universities, meanwhile, the Inter-Varsity Fellowship (later, the Universities and Colleges Christian Fellowship) ensured that Christian Unions were effective instruments of reaching the 'brightest and best' with the gospel. Student groups and churches were especially strong in Oxford and Cambridge, but generally thrived across the country.

Christian belief was also part of the wider public discourse. On the radio and in print, C S Lewis was making his unique and powerful contribution to the dialogue about faith. *The Screwtape Letters*, for example, was a perennial best-seller following its publication in 1942. And in 1954 the first visit of the American evangelist Billy Graham, whilst highly controversial because of the allegedly 'simplistic' nature of his message, brought thousands into the churches and scores if not hundreds into the ordained ministry.

Up to the 1960s, baptisms, confirmations and vocations all remained at high levels — indeed they had somewhat increased in the post-war years. 'Belief in God' was naturally assumed to mean 'belief in the *Christian* God' and 'Religious Instruction' in schools was 'instruction in the Christian religion'. Most couples were married in church, the majority had their children baptized and virtually everyone expected their funeral would be conducted by a Christian minister. Through various channels, therefore, people generally had at least some familiarity with biblical events and

Christian doctrines.

Yet Anglican evangelicals were uncertain of their place and rôle in the Church of England, particularly in the face of the advance of liberalism.

In 1963, the then-Bishop of Woolwich, John Robinson, published a small paperback, *Honest to God*, which exploded like a bombshell in both church and nation. Essentially, it was a popular summary of the kind of theology being advanced by the German giants Rudolf Bultmann, Paul Tillich and Dietrich Bonhoeffer — men whose work dominated the theological scene well into the seventies and was standard fare in universities and many theological colleges. What it suggested from a layman's perspective, however, was that many in the hierarchy of the Church of England did not believe what they seemed to be telling ordinary people *they* ought to believe.

Honest to God thus triggered something of a national crisis of faith, not so much regarding what individuals themselves believed as regarding what people thought the *Church* believed. At the same time, so-called 'situation ethics' were challenging traditional notions of a fixed morality. And it must not be forgotten that this was an era of general social upheaval, as the austerity of the post-war years gave way to the 'rock and roll' fifties and then the 'swinging' sixties.

At the same time, and partly in reaction to catholic influences, Anglican evangelicalism was itself somewhat austere and formal. For most services, evangelical clergy wore cassock, surplice, scarf and hood. Other than the CPAS material, services were entirely from the *Book of Common Prayer* and almost entirely led by the minister. The Bible was the Authorized Version, the hymnbook *Ancient and Modern*, guitars a radically 'hip' innovation and lay participation minimal. Sermons had three points and Sunday evening guest services always had an evangelistic talk.

Furthermore, many Anglican evangelicals felt themselves estranged from their parent Church. And indeed there were voices suggesting they should leave the denomination, or at least be less committed to it than to a wider evangelical fraternity.

In the face of all this, a National Evangelical Anglican Congress was convened at Keele University in 1967 to consider the future. This was a watershed, and determined the shape of the Anglican evangelical movement over the next three decades.

The Congress was not without its own internal difficulties, largely reflecting tensions between the older and younger generations. Nevertheless, the outcome was a clear and determined commitment to remain within the Church of England and to work positively with its structures. And in fact, in the next ten years Anglican evangelicalism flourished, as the hard work of the previous decades bore fruit.

Evangelical churches and para-church organizations continued to grow. Evangelical ordinands (all men at this stage, of course, and mostly in their twenties) represented an increasing proportion of the whole. Their colleges, especially St John's Nottingham under the leadership of Canon Michael Green, were at the forefront of innovation in new styles of outreach and spiritual expression. Evangelical pastoral practices, such as housegroups (which were still something of a novelty), gained in acceptability and the future looked increasingly bright for evangelicalism.

Meanwhile, the charismatic movement was developing from being virtually a 'secret society' in the sixties to mainstream in the mid-seventies, not least because of the ministry of David Watson at St Michael le Belfrey, York.

Despite the theological divisions this movement had involved (the founder of the Fountain Trust, Michael Harper, who was then curate at All Soul's Langham Place, left because of John Stott's discomfort with his charismatic leanings) it brought a freshness to music, liturgy and other expressions of church life. Music groups and drama became an established feature in many church services, banners brightened the walls of buildings, choruses replaced hymns and vibrant 'worship' (rather than long sermons) became the focus of congregational energies.

The second NEAC, at Nottingham University in 1977, gave voice to all these influences and more. Evangelicalism, it seemed, had come of age — indeed, it was now a radical, cutting-edge, force to be reckoned with. NEAC 2 was attended by over 2,000 delegates. In preparation, three books were published, each containing several essays on topics including not only the expected staples of evangelism and theology but economics, politics, international development and so on. And at the end a joint statement was agreed which represented a new benchmark of evangelical orthodoxy, signalling an interest not just in traditional 'spiritual' matters, but in every area of life.

John Stott himself was at the forefront of encouraging a new understanding of evangelical spirituality, where traditional evangelism and radical social and political engagement went hand-in-hand. And if controversy arose, he was always there to give a magisterial ruling or admonition to prevent disagreements developing into anything worse.

Within a decade, however, the evangelical movement was increasingly fragmented into conflicting camps. Worse than that, in the eyes of some, it was drifting away not just from its traditional expressions of spirituality, but from its traditional theological foundations.

Few things exemplified this more clearly, perhaps, than the history of the Greenbelt music festival, which began in the 1970s as an evangelical version of the pop festivals of the late sixties.

In the early years, Greenbelt saw itself standing in the tradition of Francis Schaeffer, Hans Rookmaker and the L'Abri Fellowship — engaged with the arts and encouraging the development of a Christian 'world view' from an essentially Calvinist and Reformed standpoint. Through the 1980s and '90s, however, the festival took greater and greater risks with the speakers it invited and the way in which topics were addressed.

Early controversy was caused when a seminar was addressed by a 'white witch', and there were further questions raised by the dress and style of dancers from the 'Nine O'Clock Service' in Sheffield (a body whose leader was later found to have been abusing members of the congregation). In the words of today's Greenbelt website,

> As the evangelical musical subculture dried up, the heart and mind of Greenbelt broadened and strengthened. Soon, artists were invited not just because they were believers or had a distant churchgoing relative, but because their vision overlapped with a biblical one of global justice (Bob Geldof) or engaging with the political powers (Midnight Oil) or was simply fuelled by a divine sense of wonder (Waterboys).[8]

Just as notable here as the change of booking policy is surely the disparaging attitude to the early years!

Today, Greenbelt is still running, and its organizers might still see themselves standing in the tradition of the founders. But, tellingly, whereas in the 1980s, the festival was covered by the more evangelical *Church of England Newspaper*, now it is given extensive space in the thoroughly liberal *Church Times*.

So once again we may ask what went wrong.

What follows is a very personal reflection, shaped by my own Anglo-catholic childhood, evangelical conversion, charismatic leanings in the seventies and eighties, and conservative re-education in the nineties. Nevertheless, I would identify the following influences leading to the fragmentation of evangelicalism.

First, the charismatic movement created amongst evangelicals an alternative identity based on shared *experience* rather than *theology*. In the 1960s and '70s, "Are you baptized in the Spirit?" was a frequent and controversial question in evangelical circles, and 'speaking in tongues' was still something of a badge of charismatic belonging. Which way you answered, therefore, and your own personal experience, determined to a large extent where and with whom you felt most comfortable.

In 1979, the first Spring Harvest took place, embracing theologically charismatic styles and speakers, and the following year saw the beginnings of the New Wine network. Evangelicals who

---

[8] http://www.greenbelt.org.uk/about/history, retrieved 20 July 2011.

were also charismatics now had somewhere to go for distinctive fellowship with their 'own kind'.

Many of those affirming their 'baptism in the Spirit', however, were from a non-evangelical background. Previously significant theological differences — even between Protestants and Roman Catholics — were being set aside in the face of a perceived 'new thing' that God was doing. David Watson himself caused controversy when he stated at the 1977 NEAC that "in many ways, the Reformation was one of the greatest tragedies that ever happened to the Church".[9] And although he later modified his comments, they reflected part of a widening evangelical spectrum.

Meanwhile, those evangelicals who had most enthusiastically embraced social and political action were becoming increasingly caught up with that agenda and rather less committed to the theological style and message of traditional evangelicalism.

In effect (though I think this suggestion would still be resisted by those who took this route), these evangelicals became rather less committed to what an earlier generation would have recognized as actual *evangelism*. Certainly the definition given in *Towards the Conversion of England* would have been regarded by them as somewhat lacking and they would have had more sympathy with the concept of 'Five Marks of Mission' developed by the Anglican Consultative Council:

1. To proclaim the Good News of the Kingdom
2. To teach, baptise and nurture new believers
3. To respond to human need by loving service
4. To seek to transform unjust structures of society
5. To strive to safeguard the integrity of creation and sustain and renew the life of the earth

Whilst there is much to commend these as expressions of Christian *concern*, however, they suffer from a lack of clarity and

---

[9] Quoted from Terry Saunders and Hugh Sansom, *David Watson, A Biography*, (Sevenoaks: Hodder & Stoughton, 1992) 179, referenced in Marshall, Thomas, *David Watson: A Legacy*, http://www.fulcrum-anglican.org.uk/page.cfm?ID=480, retrieved 20 July 2011.

coherence. In particular, it can readily be seen that direct evangelism is only referred to in general terms and is largely confined to the first two 'Marks'. The inevitable consequence is to make evangelism just a *part* of mission.

Moreover, even 'proclaiming the Good News of the Kingdom' can be given various interpretations. We often hear reference to the saying — wrongly attributed to St Francis of Assisi — "Preach the gospel at all times; if necessary, use words." (One suspects that the popularity of this dictum is directly proportional to the dislike of, or nervousness about, evangelism on the part of the speaker.) There are some, therefore, for whom 'proclaiming the Good News' will, in their view, never involve them personally having to tell anyone about Jesus.

We will return to this later. Meanwhile, however, there would be many on the evangelical spectrum who would agree with those for whom an explicit commitment to *political* action would be a *sine qua non* of a proper definition of the Church's mission to the world.

But thirdly, evangelicals generally were not well-equipped theologically and those that became more enamoured with academia frequently became less identified with traditional evangelicalism.

In the more traditionalist circles, theology was regarded as being almost incompatible with, and certainly hardly necessary to, evangelical spirituality and ministry. One manifestation of this, for example, was that evangelical ordinands were encouraged to go to the Oxford and Cambridge theological colleges, not primarily to study theology, but to engage in student ministry as a kind of 'on the job' training for parish work.

Many influential evangelicals at this stage, including John Stott, Timothy Dudley-Smith (hymnwriter, and later Bishop of Thetford), Michael Green, David Sheppard (Bishop of Liverpool) and Dick Lucas, had come through the system of Iwerne camps, started by E J Nash — and 'Bash', as he was known, was notoriously indifferent to theological training and methodology. As a result, traditional evangelical preaching and teaching tended to be somewhat simplistic and was unable to address from an explicitly *evangelical* perspective the questions being posed about spirituality and society, both from within and without the movement.

At the same time, however, other evangelical Anglicans seemed to be discovering the world of academic theology afresh. Unfortunately, the movement as a whole had no tradition of widespread academic learning integrated into a traditional local and personal evangelistic ministry. Those who developed academically therefore tended to become isolated from the constituency and, human nature being what it is, where differences developed, conflict soon resulted.

One very public demonstration of this, and an indication of when the problems had set in, was the 1983 sacking of the editorial board of *Churchman* (a journal produced by the very traditionalist Church Society) and the setting up of *Anvil* as a rival organ, in 1984. This has been briefly but ably described by Andrew Atherstone in a Latimer Study booklet.[10] From one point of view, an 'old guard' conservative inner-circle at Church Society expelled those who represented the voice of the new, theologically adventurous and confident, evangelicalism in what was effectively a palace *coup*. From another perspective, the heart of evangelicalism was saved at the last minute from an incipient liberalism. Almost thirty years later, the memories of this particular battle linger on.

By the mid 1980s, therefore, Anglican evangelicalism was no longer united in its adherence to the traditions of just two decades earlier. Yet in the short term, it was the 'new radicals' who were making the running in the movement. When the third NEAC took place, at Caister in 1988, there was a new mood in the gathering and a new style on the platform. Even the name had been changed, from 'Congress' to 'Celebration'.

Here is what Colin Day, then executive officer of the Church of

---

[10] Andrew Atherstone, *An Anglican Evangelical Identity Crisis : The Churchman-Anvil Affair of 1981-1984* (London: Latimer Trust, 2008).

England Evangelical Council, wrote at the time:

> ... NEAC 3 ... is not a simple progression [from NEACs 1 and 2].
> 'Celebration' reminds us that there is a new spirit of worship and
> confidence in the Christian world today.
>
> *Worship*, always something which Anglicans have felt strongly
> about, is to assume a much more prominent place [...]. There will be
> worship in the evening Celebration and in a variety of optional
> morning groups. *Fellowship* in small groups will centre on Bible
> study resourced by Rev Dr John Stott ... in the morning [...].
>
> There will be no Congress Statement. It isn't that sort of event. The
> statement that will be made will be one written in the hearts and
> minds of those who attend, and who will return to church and
> community to be read by those among whom they live. It will be a
> bold attempt to extricate the gospel from cerebral captivity, without
> falling into the trap of anti-intellectualism, or worse that brand of
> spiritual sensuality which is increasingly common today.[11]

As with the development of Greenbelt, we might notice again the implicit criticism of the evangelical past — the former "cerebral captivity" of the gospel being contrasted with the "spirit of worship and confidence" taken to characterize the new era. Evangelicalism had not merely 'come of age' but was moving into different territory.

Many in the evangelical Anglican constituency, however, were increasingly uncomfortable with the direction being taken by the movement, and in the mid-1980s, under the leadership of Dick Lucas at St Helen's Bishopsgate, the newly-formed Proclamation Trust struck out in a different direction.

The Proclamation Trust aimed unashamedly, and in its own mind principally, at a recovery of preaching. Nevertheless, this inevitably entailed a recovery of *theology*, and so the speakers invited to address the annual Evangelical Ministry Assembly were often men of theological acumen as well as skilled communicators.

Notably, however, most of them came from abroad — evidence if it were needed that in the UK they were in short supply. Many were from America but some, and in the end the most influential as far as Anglicans were concerned, came from the Diocese of Sydney

---

[11] Colin Day, 'NEAC 3: the celebration', *Third Way*, June 1987, 6.

in Australia.

Two leading English evangelicals at the time made some revealing comments about the impact of just one of these visitors, John Chapman, who then headed the Department of Evangelism in the Diocese of Sydney. Speaking about 'Chappo's' early influence, Jonathan Fletcher, the vicar of Emmanuel Wimbledon, commented,

> We didn't need to be encouraged in evangelism —we've always been flat out at that. We needed to be rescued for reformed theology.[12]

And Dick Lucas himself similarly said,

> When he first came to us he did a series on God and his sovereignty, and so on. I remember then being amazed at the theological nous of this man. After all, he'd come across to do evangelism and we weren't used to travelling evangelists quite like this![13]

However, although these Australians sometimes gave the impression that evangelicalism was just as embattled in Sydney as elsewhere, nothing could have been further from the truth. Rather, in Sydney, Anglican structures and evangelical theology had reached a constructive synthesis in a way far beyond the experience, or even the grasp, of most Englishmen. In hindsight, it is a shame that more was not made of this by them at the time, as it could have had a positive influence of the attitude of Anglican evangelicals here in the next two decades.

Generally, however, these links were to have an increasing influence on the English scene, not least when David Peterson, previously on the staff at Moore College in Sydney, became principal of Oak Hill Theological College in 1996. By that stage, Oak Hill was still theologically conservative but was in a seriously weakened position, having been threatened with closure in 1993 by a Church commission which was seeking to reduce the number of theological colleges and had decided that the 'pain' must be shared

---

[12] Michael Orpwood, *Chappo: For the Sake of the Gospel — John Chapman and the Department of Evangelism* (Russell Lea: Eagleswift Press, 1995) 12.

[13] *Ibid.* 12.

equally amongst the theological 'traditions'. Oak Hill was seemingly chosen not because it couldn't get the students, but because it was perceived as an 'easy target'.

On the one hand, therefore, Peterson had to fight for Oak Hill's continuing survival, sometimes against active opposition from dioceses which steered students away from the college. At the same time, however, and symptomatic of the attitude amongst conservative evangelicals, he had to fight to get the big evangelical churches to send their ordinands to him for theological training, rather than to the Oxbridge colleges to do student work.

Thus in the mid-1980s conservative Anglican evangelicalism began its own revival. At the same time, however, other evangelicals continued moving consciously away from the traditionalist camp. Tragically for the movement, the result was an increasing sense of division, which was deepened further by the events preceding the opening up of the priesthood to women in 1993.

In 1977, the Nottingham Statement produced at the second NEAC had affirmed that,

> Leadership in the church should be plural and mixed, ultimate responsibility normally singular and male.[14]

Although, as John Stott wrote in the Preface, the Statement was "not an authoritative declaration of evangelical Anglican belief", nevertheless it represented "a faithful expression of the mind of the Nottingham Congress".[15] Yet within a few years, increasing numbers of evangelicals had abandoned that position and were prepared to support a change in policy that inevitably meant women would have 'ultimate responsibility' in local church leadership. What made this particularly difficult for some of those who remained convinced of the Nottingham position was the apparent lack of theological groundwork amongst evangelicals to justify the new development.

---

[14] The Executive Committee of the Second National Evangelical Anglican Congress, *The Nottingham Statement*, para J6.

[15] *Ibid.* 4.

Evangelicals now faced a situation in which differences of conviction found a physical expression that could not be politely ignored. In response to this, one group of evangelicals set up an organization called Reform, whose stated aim was — as it happened — 'the conversion of England', but whose *raison d'être* was actually to bring together those who disagreed with the introduction of women priests.

Around this time, however, the term 'open evangelical' began to be used by those who consciously wanted to distinguish themselves from the traditionalist outlook, especially on women's ordination. As explained by the current website of Ridley Hall, Cambridge, 'open' in this sense meant being attentive to the "questions and the insights" of the world, recognizing "God's work in other Christian traditions", playing a "full part" within the Church of England and listening for God to say "new things" through the Bible and His Spirit.[16]

Yet in the years following 1993, the leadership of various evangelical bodies — notably the Church of England Evangelical Council — began to fall into the hands of those increasingly labelled by themselves and others as 'conservative' evangelicals. Partly this development was the result of them deliberately organizing themselves to stand for various vacancies. Partly it was the result of other evangelicals abandoning the old bodies and structures.

In the dioceses, for example, the local evangelical Unions and Fellowships were becoming increasingly difficult to sustain. In the immediate post-war era, any evangelical clergyman (they were, of course, all men) moving into a new diocese would be invited to, and would naturally associate himself with, the diocesan fellowship. Through the eighties and nineties, however, this could no longer be assumed. Indeed, some openly dissociated themselves from bodies seen as reminiscent of the 'marginalization' of evangelicalism. Now that the movement was being perceived by themselves as more

---

[16] 'What does "Open Evangelical" actually mean?'
http://www.ridley.cam.ac.uk/general.html#1, retrieved 20 July 2011.

integrated with the institution, the old 'evangelical huddles' were despised and neglected.

The result, though, was that an increasingly conservative rump had an influence well beyond its representative numbers in the broader evangelical constituency. The planning for a fourth National Evangelical Anglican Congress, at Blackpool in 2003, was therefore dominated by conservatives. Symptomatic of this was the return to the old name — Congress, not Celebration. Perhaps inevitably, in the run-up to the Congress there was a series of acrimonious arguments and splits, culminating in the founding behind the scenes and launch at the Congress itself of Fulcrum, a body avowedly for open evangelicals and consciously and vocally opposed to the conservatives.

Since then, events at home and in the wider Anglican Communion abroad have led to a multiplication of other groupings, notably Anglican Mainstream, the Fellowship of Confessing Anglicans and, most recently, the Anglican Mission in England (AMiE), all representing a 'traditionalist' response to perceived doctrinal and moral 'slippage'.

Meanwhile, the Church of England itself continued the steady decline which had set in at the end of the 1960s. Outwardly, it was less overtly hostile to evangelicals, and indeed numbers of them found preferment as archdeacons, cathedral deans and even diocesan bishops. However, the ethos of the institution remained a soft liberal -catholicism — middle-of-the-road in theology and fond of dressing up when it came to liturgy. Despite their increasing prominence in the institution and their continuing commitment to evangelism at the local level, evangelicals did not achieve anything like the transformation of the institution envisaged by *Towards the Conversion of England*.

Moreover, the evangelicals appointed to senior office tended to be predominantly those from the 'open' end of the spectrum. Conservative evangelicals, and specifically those opposed to the ordination of women, were seemingly much less appreciated, and it is surely unfortunate that the last episcopal appointment from their ranks was in 1997, despite the stated neutrality of the Church regarding the views held on the subject by candidates for senior appointments.[17]

What, then, is the present situation and possible future for evangelical Anglicanism?

Whereas in the 1950s evangelicals were a readily-identified and cohesive group, there is no longer any such thing as a 'mere evangelical'. Today, if you call yourself an evangelical, people in the know will immediately ask, "But what *sort* of evangelical are you?"

Thus evangelical organizations in the Church of England face serious problems in trying to hold together diverse, and even mutually hostile, versions of evangelicalism. The Church of England Evangelical Council, for example, has been repeatedly criticized, not least by members of Fulcrum, for failing to represent the 'evangelical spectrum'. Yet the CEEC is only bringing together at committee level evangelicals who today fail to coordinate and cooperate locally.[18]

Meanwhile, the more consciously *conservative* evangelicals are increasingly uncertain of their place in the Church of England. This is not only because of their anxieties over women bishops but also because of their own growing emphasis on church planting, which is often resisted by the institution or (understandably) by the parish in which a church plant takes place.

---

[17] Thus a 2007 report to the General Synod, after noting that "the proportion of women on the Preferment List [those earmarked for senior office in the Church of England] and among those holding senior appointments is lower than the proportion of full-time stipendiary clergy who are women", added that, "The proportion of minority ethnic, conservative evangelical and traditional catholic candidates ... would appear to be even lower" (GS 1650, 2007, 4.6.1,2).

[18] Stephen Kuhrt, 'Preventing CEEC from becoming a "Rump Parliament"', http://www.fulcrum-anglican.org.uk/page.cfm?ID=356, retrieved 20 July 2011 and published in *The Church of England Newspaper*, 14 November 2008. Recognizing the lack of broader evangelical involvement in traditional bodies, Kuhrt nevertheless wrote, "the current list of [CEEC] members does suggest an over-weighting in the council of conservative evangelicals and particularly those closely linked to conservative evangelical organisations."

Moreover, the younger generation of evangelicals across the spectrum have a very tentative understanding of the Church of England. The more open evangelicals seem to have little experience of or feel for past tradition exemplified by the so-called 'formularies' — the Thirty-nine Articles, the *Book of Common Prayer* and the Ordinal. The conservatives, meanwhile, seem in addition to have little commitment to the institution. And both, one suspects, are hardly aware that the Church of England has such a thing as its own doctrine — not helped by the somewhat historically cavalier attitude of the hierarchy and the casual indifference to official doctrines and practices on the part of many local clergy.

The Anglican evangelical leaders of the fifties and sixties are dying out and the next generation has not thrown up any significant replacements. Indeed, reading through a list of the younger evangelical luminaries of the 1980s, such as those who contributed to the pre-Nottingham books, it is notable how some of them would no longer identify themselves at all with the traditional evangelical constituency. Certainly there is no one like the late John Stott to whom evangelicals can look to hold them together. But in any case, there seems to be little sense of direction or coherence to the constituency.

On top of all this, society itself is increasingly hostile to Christian belief — certainly in its more conservative forms. In particular, the issue of homosexuality threatens not only to divide the Church even more but to exclude traditionalist Christians from full participation in society at many significant levels.

And yet despite everything, the Church of England is still viable.[19] It still has thousands of ministers and hundreds of thousands of members. Its parishes cover the entire nation and in some areas, particularly in the countryside, it is the only remaining visible Christian presence. It is surely worth fighting for! Indeed, it

---

[19] Though it should be noted that in some areas, particularly rural parishes, congregations are increasingly being stretched to the absolute limit meeting their financial obligations.

could still be an instrument for 'the conversion of England'.
Moreover, the problem is not — at least not primarily — the
Anglican structures. On the contrary, in many parts of the world,
such as Australia or Sub-Saharan Africa, the same structures are
enabling Church growth and driving forward evangelism. Rather,
just as in 1945, our problem on these shores is largely one of
misdirected and uncertain leadership — both local and national.

The analysis of Kenyan Bishop Samson Mwaluda as he
considered the challenges facing his diocese of Taita Taveta bear
careful consideration:

> Our experience in Kenya, as in many parts of the Anglican Church
> worldwide, is that the diocesan bishops [*sic*] leading rôle affects
> every aspect of the Church. I want to contend that one key factor in
> the reorientation of the Anglican Church in Taita Taveta for
> accelerated growth, is for the diocesan bishop to focus on his rôle as
> the chief teacher-evangelist.[20]

And he adds,

> The Anglican Church, particularly in the West, is decreasing in areas
> where bishops undervalue evangelism and the teaching of the
> apostles' doctrine. [...] Anglicanism is growing quickly where bishops
> are vision bearing evangelist-teachers ...[21]

Now it would be true to say that bishops are not the answer to all
the Church's problems. Nevertheless, we may compare Mwaluda's
statements with the contrasting attitude of the two wings of Anglican
evangelicalism.

On the one hand, there are those conservatives who treat the
episcopate virtually as an irrelevance, when in fact (as Mwaluda
observes) their attitude has a crucial effect on growth. On the other
hand, there are evangelicals who assert the fundamental importance
of the episcopate yet who do not emphasize Mwaluda's demand that
bishops be guardians of apostolic doctrine. For them, it is 'the
bishop right or wrong' which anchors their ecclesiology at this point,

---

[20] Samson Mwaluda, *Reorienting a Church for Accelerated Growth: With Special Reference to the Anglican Diocese of Taita Taveta, Kenya*, 51-52.

[21] *Ibid.* 54.

yet that is surely a defective understanding of the Church generally and Anglicanism in particular.[22]

The difference between Mwaluda and current Anglican evangelicalism in England, however, is not just over his view of the episcopate but over his understanding of a *strategy* to transform the Church into an instrument for gospel growth. To be blunt, Mwaluda *has* a strategy whereas contemporary evangelicalism does not! Theologically-conservative evangelicals see that the Church needs transformation, but have no strategy to bring this about. Institutionally-conservative evangelicals simply do not see the radical need for transformation, largely (one might suggest) because of their avowed commitment to an 'open' theological position.

Yet it is not enough to rest content that evangelicalism has improved its position in the institution — least of all when evangelicals are so divided amongst themselves. The truth is that well-placed evangelicals have not strategically used their influence to equip the Church as a whole for the task of evangelism which might lead to 'the conversion of England'.

Nor is it enough to hope that evangelicals will somehow and vaguely influence the Church of England towards somehow and unconsciously converting the nation, without confronting the uncertainties about its message and the inadequacies in its manner of life recognized as already existing in the 1940s.

Evangelicals ought to be at the forefront of evangelism. It is only a ministry which seeks conversions that deserves the label 'evangelical'. But they ought also to be aiming at nothing less than making the Church of England itself 'evangelistic'. If we are content to thrive in our small corner whilst the national Church remains

---

[22] Compare Article XXVI, 'Of the unworthiness of the Ministers, which hinders not the effect of the Sacraments': "[...] it appertaineth to the discipline of the Church that inquiry be made of evil ministers, and that they be accused by those that have knowledge of their offences; and finally, being found guilty by just judgement, be deposed." Since the bishop is charged in the Ordinal that he will "drive away all erroneous and strange doctrine contrary to God's Word; and both privately and openly ... call upon and encourage others to the same", if he does not do this he ought not to be a bishop and ought to be deposed by the Church.

indifferent to the task of evangelism, we truly care neither for our own beliefs nor for the people of our nation as a whole. In the words of Christ to the Church at Sardis, it is time to "Wake up, and strengthen what remains and is about to die" (Rev 3:2).

The rest of this booklet, therefore, will focus on presenting a strategy for the transformation of the Church of England into a body that can address the challenge identified in 1945:

> IN ENGLAND THE CHURCH HAS TO PRESENT THE
> CHRISTIAN GOSPEL TO MULTITUDES IN EVERY SECTION
> OF SOCIETY WHO BELIEVE IN NOTHING; WHO HAVE LOST A
> WHOLE DIMENSION (THE SPIRITUAL DIMENSION) OF LIFE;
> AND FOR WHOM LIFE HAS NO ULTIMATE MEANING.[23]

---

[23] *Towards the Conversion of England,* para 33.

Part 2
The Transformation of the Church: Contending for Change in the Institution

In 1995, a number of then-prominent Anglican evangelicals contributed to a book titled *Has Keele Failed?* By this they meant, has the commitment to working within the Church of England which issued from the 1967 National Evangelical Anglican Congress worked out for better or for worse?

Although dissenting voices were allowed a say, the majority view of the contributors was that things had really worked out quite well. And for many who count themselves as evangelicals today, that view continues to be the case.

Yet there are also those who believe things are worse now than at almost any time since the Second World War. The dissenting voice of the campaign group Reform (targeted by the aforementioned book) has been joined by a number of others, and there is frequent talk of a 'crisis'.

Some of these dissenters believe that traditionalist Anglicans face virtual exclusion from the institution, not least because of the consecration of women bishops. And indeed this fear is not without grounds, given the willingness of many in the leadership of the Church to renege on promises and commitments made when women were first ordained. There have been ugly scenes all round, and there are likely to be more. And of course, waiting in the wings is the perennial and divisive subject of same-sex relationships.

Yet it must also be admitted that there are some things to be grateful for from an evangelical perspective. The bench of bishops, for example, is markedly less theologically 'eccentric' and markedly more interested in church growth than even a decade ago. Admittedly, this interest is partly driven by pragmatism in the face of falling numbers. As one insider put it, "The bishops are looking into the abyss" when it comes to decline. Nevertheless, a positive interest in growth is better than no interest at all.

There has also been a decline in 'churchianity'. Churchgoing is no longer the mark of respectability that it was thirty or forty years ago. The regular Anglican churchgoer today will typically have a genuine faith, even if it is not necessarily well-informed or thought through.

Again, many parishes have adopted practices which were once the preserve of evangelicals. The Alpha Course is everywhere and to be an evangelical is no longer to be regarded as culturally or theologically eccentric.[24]

So who is right? Has Keele failed, or succeeded? To get some perspective, let us turn again to the 1945 report *Towards the Conversion of England*.

The continuing need for transformation

The key proposal of *Towards the Conversion of England* is found in the title. Its aim was conversion. Not that this was the only aim. On the contrary, there was a pressing (and what now seems almost naive) desire for moral reform as well. But the key to this was seen as being individual evangelism and, crucially, this was seen as the task of the whole Church. The instrument for the conversion of England was to be the whole Church of England, not a few parishes or clergy which happened to be keen on 'that sort of thing'.

According to the report itself, however, the Church was not up to the task. The clergy were described as poorly equipped and the laity even more so. Preaching and teaching were inadequate, and the Church was unable to confront the concerns of 'modern' society. Worst of all, many churchgoers simply had no experience of conversion themselves. Thus evangelism had to be in two directions — to the world, and to the church also, so that "the state of salvation we call conversion" would become "the usual experience of the normal Christian".[25]

---

[24] Just to be clear, I am not a great fan of the Alpha Course, specifically because of its 'two stage' approach to conversion and 'filling with the Spirit'. In the wider Church, however, despite its evangelical leanings, it would not be regarded as an evangelical preserve.

Now compare this analysis with the present situation. Certainly evangelicalism is more acceptable within the Church of England, but has the Church of England adopted an 'evangelizing' agenda? Do the business agendas of the synods and diocesan management speak about the conversion of all the people in all the parishes being the proper objective of all the clergy and of all the people under their care? Is conversion even the "usual experience" of the typical churchgoer?

The answer is surely a self-evident 'no'. Admittedly there are admirable pockets of evangelistic effort or mission initiative, but the overall picture painted in 1945 still resonates today, as anyone who reads out the relevant sections of the report to a gathering of churchgoers, as I often have, will discover. Even one of the most-trumpeted of modern initiatives, 'Fresh Expressions of Church', gives the game away in its title. It sounds dynamic and exciting, but what does it say about 'old' expressions of Church, if not that they are somewhat 'stale' and inadequate for the task?

As to evangelicals themselves, Keele succeeded in making space for them within the institution, but it did not win the institution to the 'evangelizing' agenda of 1945 — nor did it apparently aim to. Interestingly, the 1967 'Keele Statement' itself makes no reference to *Towards the Conversion of England*,[26] and the work of evangelism is almost treated as if it were the sole responsibility of evangelicals.

There are clear aspirations for the Church as a whole. In one place, for example, the Statement says,

> We urge that dioceses will designate special mission areas, calling for support from the wider Church, and the maximum flexibility in matters of organisation and liturgy.[27]

Yet overall, the tone is one of low expectations for the wider

---

[25] *Towards the Conversion of England*, para 81.

[26] Charles Yeats, *Has Keele Failed?: Reform in the Church of England* (London: Hodder & Stoughton, 1995), 173-209.

[27] *Ibid.* 183.

Church of England. At the same time, there is a certain amount of 'breast beating' regarding perceived evangelical failures. The nett effect is to urge more change from evangelicals than from the wider institution — which arguably is exactly what happened. Thus, for example, evangelicals became much more 'sacramentalist' in the years following Keele, with services of Holy Communion becoming more frequent and more central to Sunday activities.

Yet given the lack of any practical suggestions for changing the denomination, it is unsurprising that the changes were largely in one direction.

Indeed, thanks to its own divisions, the evangelical constituency is arguably in a worse position today than in 1967. Conservative evangelicals can see the problems in the institution and the need for evangelistic initiatives, but their only new strategy has been to encourage church-planting. The less-conservative, on the other hand, seem happy to pursue their own local agenda, but lack much evident concern about institutional problems and issues.

Meanwhile, the wider Church of England remains largely non-evangelical both in its theology and its missiology.[28] Church growth is becoming more popular, but personal conversion is as uncomfortable an issue now as it was in 1945.

Reasserting evangelism

The transformation of the Church of England must begin, then, with a reassertion of evangelism — but this will also entail a critical examination of our understanding of 'the gospel'.

We referred earlier to the 'Five Marks of Mission', which have come to function as an unofficial, but highly popular, summary of the Church's *raison d'être*. The adoption of these 'Marks of Mission', however, has had serious consequences for the Church.

Thus, Martin Davie, in his *A Guide to the Church of England*, asserts on this basis that, "the Church of England ... sees mission as

---

[28] Missiology is the doctrine of mission.

something that involves more than simply evangelism."[29]

Indeed Davie explicitly critiques the definition of evangelism used in *Towards the Conversion of England*, quoting with approval the words of Paul Avis:

> ... mission is bigger than evangelization. Evangelization is a *part* of which mission is the *whole*. As Moltmann puts it, '[...] Evangelization is mission, but mission is not merely evangelization.'[30]

The problem with this analysis is that it has been rejected by a subsequent Anglican body set up to continue the study of mission: the 'Standing Commission for Mission of the Anglican Communion', also known as MISSIO. According to its report on the Anglican Communion official website,

> At its second meeting (Ely 1996), MISSIO began reviewing the 'Five Marks of Mission' as developed by the Anglican Consultative Council between 1984 and 1990. We recognise with gratitude that the Five Marks have won wide acceptance among Anglicans, and have given parishes and dioceses around the world a practical and memorable "checklist" for mission activities.
>
> However, we have come to believe that, as our Communion travels further along the road towards being mission-centred, the Five Marks need to be revisited.[31]

Crucially, and *contra* the assertions of Davie, Avis and indeed Jurgen Moltmann, the report goes on to say,

> The first mark of mission, identified at ACC-6 with personal evangelism, *is really a summary of what all mission is about*, because it is based on Jesus' own summary of his mission (Matthew 4:17, Mark 1:14-15, Luke 4:18, Luke 7:22; cf. John 3:14-17). Instead of being just one (albeit the first) of five distinct activities, *this should*

---

[29] Martin Davie, *A guide to the Church of England* (London: Mowbray, 2008) 204.

[30] *Ibid.* 204. Interestingly, although Davie quotes the definition of evangelism used in *Towards the Conversion of England*, he seems to rely entirely on Avis for this, who refers only to the original 1918 Archbishops' Committee. In his own short historical summary of 'The Church of England and Mission', Davie makes no mention of the report whatsoever — a further indication of how completely it has been forgotten and neglected.

[31] http://www.anglicancommunion.org/ministry/mission/fivemarks.cfm, retrieved 26 September 2011.

be the key statement about everything we do in mission. (Emphasis added)[32]

In other words, far from personal evangelism being a *part* of mission, it is (properly understood) the very *heart* of mission.

The reason for this will hopefully become clear if we look carefully at the definition of evangelism used in *Towards the Conversion of England.*

This states carefully and explicitly that to evangelize is "so to present Christ Jesus in the power of the Holy Spirit, that men shall come to put their trust in God through Him, to accept Him as their Saviour, and serve Him as their King". The last point, however, is often missed, even by those doing the evangelism.

Personally I find some difficulties (not to say confusion) in the ideas about justification being put forward by the former Bishop of Durham, Tom Wright, and in some of the applications he suggests of the significance of the resurrection. However, I believe he is spot-on when he says that evangelism ought to be the announcement of the lordship of Christ:

> ... 'the gospel', in the New Testament, is the good news [...] that Jesus, whom ... God raised from the dead, is the world's true Lord.[33]

Our problem has been with the extent of Christ's lordship. Undoubtedly this is in part because of our own sinfulness and the pervasiveness of sin in the world, which makes us unable to see what his lordship requires and unwilling to be obedient when we finally understand. In the former nations of Western Christendom it may also have been because the government and the laws did some of the work for us. Today, however, the challenge is perhaps greater than ever, and pastors must work harder to show what it means.

Crucially, we must see that evangelism does not consist simply of calling people to 'get right with God', but, through a right relationship with God, to 'get right with our neighbour'.

Moreover, to serve Christ as King is not just a matter of tweaking

---

[32] *Ibid.*

[33] Tom Wright, *Surprised by Hope* (London: SPCK, 2007) 238

our personal morality (mostly in the area of family life and sexuality), but in bringing every aspect of our lives under his rule *and* in extending his rule as far as possible into every area of life over which we have any influence.

Historically, we can find radical examples of English Christians doing just this in business life and in the political arena— unfortunately they are not usually the Anglicans! Nevertheless, there are surely lessons to be learned from how, for example, the Quakers who set up Boots the Chemists treated their workers.

Some may ask how this differs from the way that evangelicals in the 1970s and '80s moved into areas like politics and social action. The answer is that we must see and show that our actions in this regard flow directly and explicitly from our obedience to the Christ who calls *everyone* to acknowledge him as Lord. We must ensure that, in the words of the Sermon on the Mount, people see our good works and glorify our Father who is in heaven. Our actions must be *the natural basis for proclamation* because they are themselves the fruits of obedience to the gospel.

Regarding the Church, therefore, we must not allow evangelism to be reduced to a 'part' of mission. It is sad to see as distinguished a theologian as Moltmann quoted saying that mission is "not merely evangelization" — as if there were anything 'mere' about the proclamation that Christ is Lord and the calling on people to obey his kingship. In the Church of England today as whole, however, that is often how evangelism is seen, and it is not long before it is reduced from being a *part* of mission to being an *optional extra* in mission.

But equally, we must not allow evangelism to be reduced to a personal call to change our views as to whether or not we believe in God and what we believe about ourselves and about Jesus dying for our sins. We cannot have Christ as Saviour if we will not have Christ as Lord. And his lordship must extend into every area of the lives of those whom he saves. There is a challenge here for the more conservative evangelical. But the conservative evangelical is also entitled to ask what has happened, institutionally, to the call to personal conversion.

Once again, nothing less than an institutional transformation is required, which needs a deliberate and conscious strategy. And therein lies our problem. Evangelicals will generally go on evangelizing, whatever happens in the wider institution. But this will not lead to a programme suitable to the conversion of England. That needs a bolder and more ambitious approach, yet at present there is no sign of that coming from the official, hierarchical, leadership. Given where we are today, then, how can we address the need for the transformation of the Church?

Transforming our attitude

There are essentially two ways under God in which the Church of England might be transformed. One is from above, the other from below.

Historically, the Church of England has been rather better at the former than the latter. The Reformation, for example, was initially driven by the governing authorities of the Church using legal instruments, as was the re-institution of the old Anglican structures at the Restoration.

But this has not always been the case. The Oxford Movement, in particular, was a transformation from below, relying on principled, radical (and often illegal!) actions by ordinary clergy and laity.[34]

It seems at the moment that we are left with little choice other than a similar 'bottom up' approach, and this attracts many evangelicals to the notion of principled, radical, and even illegal, actions.

Yet had the proposals of *Towards the Conversion of England* been followed through, the transformation would have been 'top

---

[34] The two books to read are John Reed, *Glorious Battle: The Cultural Politics of Victorian Anglo-Catholicism* (London: Tufton Books, 1998) and James C Whisenant, *A Fragile Unity: Anti-ritualism and the Division of Anglican Evangelicalism in the Nineteenth Century* (Milton Keynes: Paternoster Press, 2004)

down', with the authorities within the Church providing the leadership and direction. And as experience elsewhere demonstrates, this can be a happier (and is surely a more logical) alternative to uncomfortably-driven change from below. After all, it is surely the rôle of leadership to lead, and who is better placed than the official leaders to do this?

This latter realization, however, may itself suggest an approach which embraces both 'alternatives' — change driven from below and from above. Like Nathan with David, evangelicals could adopt a 'prophetic' model in relation to the institution — reminding it of what, under God, it ought to be doing. The necessary presupposition is that things *could* get better. Nathan's words to David encouraged him to be the godly king. Jesus' words to the seven churches in Revelation encouraged them to be faithful. The epistles are full of encouragements to various congregations and individuals.

There must, of course, be the willingness to confront — but biblical confrontation generally aims at evoking positive change, even in the worst of circumstances. Thus, Nathan's famous "You are the man" (2 Sam 12:7) identifies David as an adulterer and murderer, yet it is accompanied by words of forgiveness (2 Sam 7:13) which lead ultimately to repentance (Ps 51) which are a pattern for subsequent generations. Similarly, each of the letters to the churches in Revelation 2-3 contains a promise "To him who overcomes". Despite the dire nature of some of these congregations, Jesus still speaks to them and still looks for change.

To take this approach will involve a significant change of expectation on the part of many Anglican evangelicals. Here, however, the specifically *English* experience is generally unhelpful. Many English evangelicals assume that 'the diocese' will always be the enemy, that bishops will always be a let-down, and so on. Yet in Africa and other areas of the world, things work very differently for the good of both the Church and the wider community. Those of us who have experience in the wider Communion have a special part to play in this change of attitude.

In order to change the Church, then, it is necessary to believe that the Church can be changed and therefore to have a positive attitude to the institution. Yet at the same time, those who want to change the Church must also be ready and able to confront the institution. The prophet must speak both positively *and* critically. And this, again, is where evangelicals have faced difficulties.

Recent evangelical confrontation has been either from a position of 'trench warfare' or 'ghettoization'. Many evangelical commentators have characterized the period up to the 1980s as the former, and some would see the period since then, at least for conservatives, as representing the latter. In the 'trench warfare' period, evangelicals saw themselves as an embattled, faithful minority defending the truth against the assaults of Anglo-catholicism and liberalism. And, as we saw earlier, there was a lot to justify this mentality, particularly in the 1960s and '70s. Some would also link this with a greater sense of evangelical unity, inspired by the perception of a common enemy.

Since the relative expansion of evangelicalism in the 1980s, however, evangelicals have been clearly less united amongst themselves. Those that still felt estranged from the institution have become even more isolated, withdrawing into ghettos of successful (or at least, well-defended) congregational life. For them, confrontation has been a matter of hostility to much of what the institutional Church represents and isolation from its structures. The less-conservative, on the other hand, having hit on the label 'open evangelical', are seemingly unwilling to confront the institution.

In point of fact, however, neither attitude is adequate to the challenge, since either way the vast majority of the Church of England is left untouched and therefore the vast majority of the country unevangelized.

For some in the evangelical camp, then, the need is actually to have the courage of their convictions. It has often been observed, for example, that since the 1970s there has been an increasing number of evangelical diocesan bishops. That may be true, but we might reasonably ask whether this has left any diocese discernibly more 'evangelistic' as a result. One response might be this is not the bishop's rôle — that the bishop is to be 'bishop' to the whole diocese, and cannot therefore favour one 'tradition' above another. But if we are thinking of these issues principally in terms of 'traditions' we are already starting from the wrong place.

The mission of the Church is given in the Great Commission: "Go and make disciples of all nations." Therefore the task of the bishop is to fulfil the Great Commission and, in its furtherance, to encourage what is conducive to that goal and to correct what is not.

We cannot excuse a failure to engage in this mission on the grounds of maintaining a tradition that "We don't do evangelism." The *institutional* problem with this is that the Church of England divides the world into geographical 'parishes', and there are rules and expectations about what outsiders can and (more importantly) can't do in those areas. Thus if the local congregation doesn't 'do conversion', then strictly speaking no one else who is Anglican can either.

It is only the bishop who can really address this issue — and in fact has considerable legal powers, including the use of a Bishop's Mission Order, which would enable him to do just that.[35] Specifically, it is the bishop's job to ask why mission is not taking place (if that is indeed the case).

At the moment, however, few bishops seem willing to grasp this particular nettle. Indeed, to judge from official documents to do with the selection and training of ordination candidates, the willingness to accept any and every variant calling itself Anglican is a key requirement for the Church's ministry.[36]

---

[35] See http://www.churchofengland.org/clergy-office-holders/pastoralandclosedchurches/pastoral/bmos.aspx

[36] Thus the second major 'criterion' identified in the document, 'Criteria for Selection for Ordained Ministry in the Church of England approved by The House of Bishops, to be used from September 2010', states that, "Candidates should show an understanding of their own tradition within the Church of England, an awareness of the diversity of traditions and practice, and a commitment to learn from and work generously with difference."

Case Study: *'giving as partners'*

One of the most frustrating aspects of institutional Church life is the kind of financial arrangement known as 'quota' or 'parish share', which essentially 'taxes' financially viable parishes to maintain ministry across the rest of a diocese.[37] In some cases, this diocesan 'quota' means that the minority of parishes are quite literally supporting the majority.[38]

In reaction, some of these better-off parishes have proposed 'capping', or even cutting, such quota payments. Almost inevitably, however, this prompts accusations of failing to be 'team players' or even of not being 'truly Anglican'. Yet there is usually no corresponding willingness on the part of diocesan authorities to ask why other parishes are not paying their way in terms of covering their ministry costs. Nor is there any acknowledgement that giving parishes feel deeply concerned about money being wasted.

A few years ago, I devised a workable proposal whereby parishes could meet the central request for 'quota' whilst making sure that funds were channelled to ministries of their choice within a diocese. Titled Giving as Partners, *or* GAP, *it acknowledged the need for mutual support but also the need for mutual accountability in the mission and ministries that were being supported.[39]*

The scheme used an existing accounting provision within the funding arrangements for clergy paid centrally by the Church Commissioners, and over the brief period for which it operated, was shown to work. The fact that it

---

[37] For a cogent critique of such financial structures by a diocesan 'insider' see Bob Jackson, *The Road to Growth: Towards a Thriving Church* (London: Church House, 2005).

[38] This was certainly true at one stage in my own diocese, Chelmsford.

[39] The explanatory booklet can still be downloaded from the Church Society website here: http://www.churchsociety.org/publications/leaflets/Leaf_GivingAsPartners.pdf

was not immediately popular at 'diocesan' level also suggests that its deeper implications about the 'balance of power' were recognized.

The real problem, in the end, was that those who most explicitly demanded change in the system were dissatisfied that the proposal did not withhold money from dioceses or 'punish' them in any way. And the fact that this wasn't its purpose left them baffled!

In the end, the scheme folded for lack of participants, but it showed what could be done simply and without generating too much antagonism, if there was the will.

One of the greatest initial challenges is going to be persuading the institution that seeking the conversion of the nation should be the practical priority for the Church and that this requires far-reaching transformation. Nothing has significantly changed in this regard since 1945.

This is why the AEJCC adopted a 'twin track' approach of transformation *and* proclamation. We cannot simply sit by and do nothing when people are not hearing the gospel. Hence even actions like irregular church-plants may still be envisaged and supported. But there is a difference between thumbing one's nose at the institution and calling for institutional repentance and transformation. If we believe in the Church of England at all, we must believe the best for it. And if we expect it to be transformed, we must act as if transformation were possible.

Transforming our local ministry

The place where transformation must begin is in our local ministry. Here, however, we must face the fact that many Anglican evangelicals are definitely 'Anglican Lite'. And this itself may be a barrier to the 'conversion of England'.

The attitude taken to the 'occasional offices' (the services of baptism, marriage and burial) can be especially significant. Since these can make substantial demands on their time, some clergy regard them more as an imposition than an opportunity, and who can blame them? Families who come for baptism often seem to be more interested in the party afterwards than the promises they make on behalf of their children. Couples spend vast amounts on their wedding, but between the bride walking down the aisle and the two of them parading out, the service itself is almost an interruption in the day. In any case, it makes little practical difference as they are usually living together. As to funerals, this is usually the first contact with a family, and typically the last.

Yet to neglect the occasional offices is to cut ourselves off from the local community whose members look to the Church of England at these points in their lives. By the very nature of our society, we cannot afford to become known as 'the church that likes to say no' if we are to promote the conversion of England.

This is especially true in rural areas, where expectations of the Church are still very traditional. Despite the fact that people come with the wrong attitude and may indeed (at least at the outset) be just using the Church for their own convenience, we have the opportunity either to meet them where they are or to put them off for ever. There were people who came to Jesus with the wrong attitude, but they all went away with something — even if it was only an awareness that what he was offering wasn't what they wanted.

Peter Bolt's little booklet, *Mission Minded*, rightly highlights the need for 'raising awareness' as part of the process of evangelism.[40] Our need is to see that the occasional offices fit entirely into that pattern.

Funerals, in particular, provide regular opportunities to speak to an attentive audience about eternal life, our need for forgiveness, Jesus' death for our sins, how we cannot get to God except through him and how we must ask him for help. Often the congregation

---

[40] Peter Bolt, *Mission Minded: A Tool for Planning Your Ministry Around Christ's Mission* (Kingsford NSW: St Matthias Press, 1992).

consists of those whom we would struggle to get into our Sunday services.

But this is why simply 'going through the motions', even in a warm and positive way, is not enough After all, the Church of England has been practising this ministry for centuries, and yet how often has it borne evangelistic fruit? Some of those involved need to read again (or perhaps read for the first time) the Prayer Book *Ordinal* and see what it says about the work of the minister:

> ... ye are called ... to be messengers, watchmen, and stewards of the Lord; to teach and to premonish, to feed and provide for the Lord's family; to seek for Christ's sheep that are dispersed abroad, and for his children who are in the midst of this naughty world, that they may be saved through Christ for ever.

The occasional offices are not an opportunity for us to show how welcoming or 'inclusive' we are. They are a means through which we may "seek Christ's sheep". If we are going to use them effectively, therefore, we must approach them with *urgency*, not simply fulfilling people's requirements from us, but seeking through this means to make Jesus known to them.

Sometimes, it is true, clergy are confronted by so many demands for the occasional offices that they cannot possibly use them all to the full. But this is surely the point at which a congregation needs to be encouraged to develop its own resources. Training others to do something is always more time-consuming than doing it yourself, yet aren't these exactly the sorts of challenges and opportunities we ought to be confronting?

Case Study: growth through the occasional offices

An Australian colleague of mine is brilliant at using the occasional offices evangelistically. In our benefice, couples go through Christianity Explored as a baptism preparation course, but my colleague has also developed his own material for wedding preparations and is assiduous in visiting before and after funerals.

> The congregation he mostly supervises meets at 8.45 on
> a Sunday morning in a traditional church building without
> any kitchen, toilet or other facilities. The services alternate
> weekly between Morning Prayer and Holy Communion,
> both from the Book of Common Prayer. The congregation
> are generally the over-55s, the building is not particularly
> warm, the seating is traditional pews and at Holy
> Communion there is no music.
>
> This congregation, however, has seen more growth than
> any in our Benefice, and much of this is down to his use of
> the occasional offices — that and their own positive and
> welcoming attitude.

A 'rigorist' approach regarding the occasional offices can have the effect of putting people off the Church entirely, whilst a *laissez faire* acceptance of all comers leaves those involved complacent and unchallenged. The offices can be a real vehicle of mission if (and only if) they are approached as providing an opportunity for evangelism.

Of course, if we were starting from scratch, we would not choose to do things this way — offering overtly Christian liturgical occasions to an all-too-frequently non-Christian clientele. But we are not starting from scratch and our attitude to the offices says a lot about our attitude to our denomination and its place in our society.[41] As to the transformation of the Church, evangelicals could and should be leading the way in this area.

Affirming the denomination

Many conservative evangelicals, however, take a distinctively negative view of the whole idea of the denomination. After all, it is argued, in the New Testament we find only two manifestations of

---

[41] In any case, it needs to be observed that Anglican clergy cannot refuse baptism to any child in their parish for whom it is requested. Nor, except in limited circumstances, can they refuse to marry or conduct a funeral for anyone living in the parish.

'church' — the physical, local, congregation and the transcendent, universal, body of Christ.

Indeed, the denomination defined as a formal division of the Church along conflicting and competing theological lines would have been an anathema to the Apostles and is utterly contrary to what Jesus intended. We can just imagine Paul asking, "Was Cranmer crucified for you? Were you baptized into the name of Calvin?" And did not Jesus himself say of his disciples at the Last Supper, "May they be brought to complete unity to let the world know that you sent me" (Jn 17:23)?

It is salutary to notice this emphasis on unity throughout the New Testament. And yet this is actually a good starting point for considering the denomination in a positive light, since it reminds us that unity was always more than 'congregational'.

In Acts 15, for example, the Council at Jerusalem is not an entirely happy occasion, nor are its decisions the last word on the subject of Gentile inclusion. Nevertheless, it took place on the clear understanding that all the parts of the Church have a responsibility towards one another and that 'local' churches cannot simply go their own way, regardless of the rest.

In this respect, therefore, denominations rightly look for unity at a wider level than the local congregation. The problem (as the Church of Rome is fond of pointing out) is not their desire for unity but their division from one another. Ideally, there really ought to be just one, united, Church. Following the Reformation, however, formal divisions became acceptable to Protestants and have been multiplying ever since.

Nevertheless, in the sixteenth century the Church of England regarded itself as a continuation of the universal 'catholic' Church. What distinguished it from other Churches was not doctrine but geography. Otherwise, it was meant to be simply 'what it said on the tin': *the* Church, *of* England. Thus in his preface to the 1552 *Book of Common Prayer*, Archbishop Thomas Cranmer declared,

And in these our doings we condemn no other Nations, nor prescribe any thing but to our own people only; For we think it convenient that

> every Country should use such Ceremonies as they shall think best
> to the setting forth of God's honour and glory, and to the reducing of
> the people to a most perfect and godly living ...

Here is not the place to go into detail, but the concept of the "particular or national Church" (Article XXXIV) is fundamental to the English Reformation. In the view of the English Reformers, the reason that there could be a 'Church of England' at all was *not* that other Churches had got it wrong (though some certainly had),[42] but that England was an independent 'empire' with its own king and therefore could make its own decisions about "ceremonies or rites of the Church ordained only by man's authority".[43] Otherwise, the doctrines of the Church of England were meant to be universal (ie catholic):

> The Church hath power to decree Rites or Ceremonies, and
> authority in Controversies of Faith: and yet it is not lawful for the
> Church to ordain any thing that is contrary to God's Word written ...
> (Article XX, 'Of the Authority of the Church')

Although it is clearly an optimistic assessment, Bishop Stephen Neill's summary nevertheless represents the Anglican ideal:

> The Church of England is the Catholic Church in England. It teaches
> all the doctrines of the Catholic Faith, as these are to be found in
> Holy Scripture, as they are summarized in the Apostles', the Nicene,
> and the Athanasian Creeds, and set forth in the dogmatic decisions
> of the first four General Councils of the undivided Church. Firmly
> based on the Scriptures as containing all things necessary to
> salvation, it still throws out its challenge: 'Show us that there is
> anything clearly set forth in Holy Scripture that we do not teach and
> we will teach it. Show us that anything in our teaching or practice is
> clearly contrary to Holy Scripture, and we will abandon it.'[44]

---

[42] See Article XIX: "As the Church of *Jerusalem*, *Alexandria*, and *Antioch* have erred: so also the Church of *Rome* hath erred, not only in their living and manner of ceremonies, but also in matters of faith." But notice these are all geographical locations!

[43] See the Act of Supremacy, 1534. An indispensable resource for students of this period is Gerald Bray, *Documents of the English Reformation* (Cambridge: James Clarke & Co Ltd, 2004).

[44] Stephen Neill, *Anglicanism* (Harmondsworth: Penguin,1965), 417. Note, however, that the Articles of Religion keep open the possibility that even such Councils as Neill refers to may have erred. In the end, Scripture alone is the final Anglican criterion by which things may be judged.

Obviously this is only an aspiration. Few people today would argue that the Church of England fully lives up to the standard it sets out. Nevertheless, at its best the way we do things in the Church of England is our historically-rooted attempt to be faithful to the word of God as it applies in our situation.

At the same time, if we are to engage with the Church for its transformation, we must both recognize and accept as a starting point that the way the Church of England does things is not a perfect match for what we discern in the New Testament.

You cannot, for example, simply overlay the Anglican orders of deacons, priests and bishops on the pages of Scripture and find a match at every point. For some, this is evidence of the importance of tradition. According to them, priesthood as we know it emerged under the guidance of the Spirit, along a trajectory established by the Apostles. For some evangelicals, on the other hand, it is an aberration which should be challenged by using the word 'presbyter' rather than 'priest'.

Whatever our view, however, what we have in place *now* is how we currently do things, even though it may not be perfect. Importantly, therefore, our assessment of this and similar issues should take into account whether current practice is intended to produce a 'New Testament' outcome consistent with the gospel and conducive to its proclamation, even if it does not precisely replicate New Testament structures. We do not, for example have a roll of widows, as in 1 Timothy 5:9, but provided we care for the widows, we are arguably no worse off for that and no less 'biblical'.

However, the Anglican 'structural framework' is much more than the orders of ministry. It extends in one direction through the managerial and administrative bodies of the institution, the office workers as well as the 'officers', and the diocesan committees as well as the Synods. Just as importantly, as we have seen already, it extends in the other direction to include the way that the Church of England is 'embedded' in the community.

Go anywhere in the country, and you will see physical evidence of Anglicanism. And despite 'secularization', the Church of England still has a place in the national 'psyche'. People with little faith and no Church affiliation still come to the Church of England to get married, to have their children baptized and their dead buried. There is an expectation of us to which we must respond in one way or another.

We can choose either to detach ourselves from, or involve ourselves in, these aspects of denominational life. Involvement certainly risks compromise. But detachment simply abandons the institution and society and accepts the creation of our own ghettos.

To affirm the denomination is not at all to approve everything for which it stands, or everything it does now or has done in the past. It is a 'warts and all' willingness to recognize, despite its imperfections, that the Anglican way of doing things has a place and that we have a place in it. Only with this attitude, however, do we have the possibility, and the right, to seek deep change in the institution.

Securing the local congregation

The transformation of the denomination, then, must begin with the local church. And despite efforts by some to define this as the diocese,[45] as far as Anglican practice is concerned, 'local churches' are actually the congregations that meet together and build their lives in Christ together, usually gathering in the parish church building and usually doing so on a weekly basis.

This view is supported by the Thirty-nine Articles, which identify the "visible church" as,

> ... a congregation of faithful men, in the which the pure Word of God is preached and the sacraments be duly ministered according to Christ's ordinance ... (Article XIX, 'Of the Church').

---

[45] See Paul Avis, *The Anglican Understanding of the Church: An Introduction* (London: SPCK, 2000).

Those who want to argue that this means the diocese point out that the Latin version of the Article uses a term for 'congregation' (*coetibus*) which properly applies to the *whole* people of God, not just a part. This is true, but the 'visible' element is fundamental to the interpretation and application of the Article. It is where the word and the sacraments are *actually* preached and administered that the Church is made visible. And that does not happen at a 'diocesan' level.[46]

As the same Article indicates, moreover, the life of the local church is secured by the ministry of the word.[47] Traditionally, evangelicals have thought of themselves as strong on this point, but there is room for improvement.

Our preaching, for example, is often nowhere near as good as we like to think. Like any professionals, clergy ought periodically to expose their preaching to peer assessment. Years ago, I regularly went on conferences for this purpose organized by the Proclamation Trust, where Dick Lucas would critique my latest attempts at biblical exposition. To my recollection, he never said anything nice, but I learned more from his negative comments than from any praise I have ever received! All of us could do with just such a 'reality check' on occasion.

Case Study: developing and using a preaching team
Some decades ago, a former vicar of our benefice, with the permission of the diocesan bishop (an important point) set up a lay-preaching team. Rather than being sent on official training courses, they were chosen and developed within the benefice.

---

[46] In fact, if the Article refers to the 'universal' church, the limitation of this to the 'local' Anglican diocese is itself artificial. Paul Avis does so because he wants to give preeminence to the bishop, but this also involves the notion that local ministry is an extension of the bishop's ministry — a doctrine which understandably finds some support amongst bishops, but ought to be resisted as unbiblical by the Church.

[47] 'Sacramental' ministry is best understood as a special instance of the 'ministry of the word'.

Today that team continues, even though only one of the original members is still active. As people within the benefice have shown potential talent for preaching, so we have given them an opportunity to become involved. The team meets once a month when we review matters and usually have some teaching input. Where possible, individuals are also given feedback on their preaching by a member of the clergy.

The most obvious result is that we are able to run five services most Sundays without being over-stretched. However, the existence of the preaching team also gives us opportunities to minister in other churches during vacancies or when staff are on holiday.

When such requests occurred in the past, we used to send one of the lay preachers along. Today, we are more likely to send one of the clergy who can also lead the service. In this way, we try to exemplify 'best practice' in the liturgy as well as in preaching and teaching from the Bible. Quite often, this is commented on by congregation members, who are not used to hearing God's word this way.

But we also need to see that the 'ministry of the word' goes beyond pulpit preaching. Sometimes evangelical ministers forget the importance of the personal aspects of ministry — getting to know people as individuals and visiting them at home. Some of the 'heroes' of the past were prodigious visitors. At very least, clergy need to set an example to the congregation of caring about people. Visiting the sick, for example, is time well-spent if it shows that we care for people at every stage of life's journey.

Furthermore, we need reminding that the purpose of preaching is not (as I have heard said) 'to teach the Bible accurately'. Certainly we should aim at this, but the real purpose, as Dr Peter Adam has pointed out, is so that people's lives may be conformed to the pattern of Christ, and there are many ways of doing this in addition to the pulpit.[48] Despite our sense of confidence, if we look at the outcome in people's understanding and their manner of life, evangelical Anglican ministry often leaves much to be desired.

And yet we are right to keep the ministry of the word at the centre. The Prayer Book Ordinal addresses deacons who are about to be ordained priest in terms which underline this point:

> And seeing that you cannot by any other means compass the doing of so weighty a work, pertaining to the salvation of man, but with doctrine and exhortation taken out of the holy Scriptures, and with a life agreeable to the same; consider how studious ye ought to be in reading and learning the Scriptures, and in framing the manners both of yourselves, and of them that specially pertain unto you, according to the rule of the same Scriptures: and for this self-same cause, how ye ought to forsake and set aside (as much as you may) all worldly cares and studies.

If the individual is the 'living stone' from which the Church is constructed (1 Pet 2:5), the word of God is the means by which that construction takes place (1 Cor 3:1-13). We are therefore right to be concerned with this ministry above all things, and to be careful that those who are under our care receive and practice only what is truly edifying in this regard.

Involving the local congregation locally

In order to transform the Church of England, we must be ready and willing to move beyond our congregations. The local church is not simply to be defended against the denomination, but ought to be involved in its transformation. Unfortunately, local congregations are often ignorant of the national and international issues affecting the Church. Indeed, as a general rule, the more conservative the minister, the less the congregation seems to know or care about matters outside its own parish.

Yet we expect our congregations to care about bringing the gospel to far-flung corners of the globe. Why should they not then

---

[48] Peter Adam, *Hearing God's Words: Exploring Biblical Spirituality* (Nottingham: IVP, 2004).

care about the progress of the gospel in the parish next door, or in the national Church? Most of them, however, scarcely know even to what diocese they belong. Their attitude is often one of happy isolation, glad that they are 'not like other Anglicans, and especially those people in the neighbouring non-evangelical parish'.

Now of course (as was recognized in 1945) there are indeed problems in the wider Church — perhaps even in the next door parish. Many clergy are indifferent to the task of evangelism and many parishioners are confused and even complacent. But the answer is not to alienate ourselves even further from them.

Nor is it automatically the answer to plant a church in the other parish, tempting though that may be. Quite simply, few congregations have the resources to do this. Moreover, church planting is fraught with difficulties, needing careful leading and nurturing. In any case, if there is a parish next door, there is technically already a church of sorts planted there, even if it is as much in need of rebuke and reform as any of the churches addressed in the book of Revelation.

From a tactical point of view, therefore, one option is to encourage good people who go to an evangelical church but who live in another parish to join in with congregational life in that other church as well, rather than trying to get them to start a rival congregation under an Anglican banner. Of course there will be struggles and difficulties, but there are going to be those anyway. The fundamental thing will be for the supporting congregation to nurture those same people in their involvement, which may include meeting with them on a regular basis or having them also attend their 'sending' church for fellowship.

However, by becoming members of the parish church where they live, joining its electoral roll and so on (and you can be a member of two electoral rolls), they have 'permission' to do other things in that parish — to get involved in the baptisms, weddings and funeral follow-up, for example, or in visiting and nurturing new arrivals in the area. They could even run a home Bible study group. Above all, they can befriend members of that congregation, get alongside them and encourage them in their Christian life and walk.

Case Study: dual church involvement

A couple from an evangelical congregation has been faithfully ministering for many years in their local church in the village where they actually live, despite the non-evangelical nature of that church.

This has been challenging for them, as they have been severely restricted regarding what they are allowed to do. Nevertheless, they have persisted in this, even whilst regularly attending services in another village several miles away where there is an evangelical Anglican ministry.

As a result of their commitment, they have the respect of their fellow parishioners and have been able to introduce, albeit in a low-key way, helpful elements to the services and the life of the parish. One of them has also been able to serve on the Parochial Church Council and therefore to influence the church positively at this level.

There will be those, of course, for whom this 'softly, softly' approach will seem too slow, and that is understandable. But the fact is that such an approach has never really been used tactically by the evangelical constituency as a whole and so we have not really seen how effective it might be if systematically applied.

Our own 'parochialism' means that we have not really thought through how to influence other congregations in a deliberate way. Yet *Towards the Conversion of England* spoke of the need for evangelism "within as well as without the Church". We ought, then, to be considering how to put that into effect.

In the Church of England, moreover, parishes are grouped into larger administrative areas called 'deaneries'. Each deanery has a senior minister called the Rural Dean (the Area Dean in some urban settings), and has a Deanery Synod, to which representatives of local churches are elected by their electoral roll members.

Increasingly, especially in the countryside, these deaneries are taking on a rôle in governance and in mission strategy. Yet typically, evangelical clergy and parishes look down on them and avoid getting involved. This was understandable twenty or thirty years ago, when deaneries were largely a practical irrelevance, but it is a significant mistake to continue with this attitude today.

Deaneries actually provide another opportunity to influence the wider denomination. By turning up at deanery chapter meetings (the gathering of local clergy), evangelicals get known by, as well as get to know, their fellow ministers, and out of this can come opportunities to preach in other churches or to bring an evangelical perspective into joint activities. For many laypeople in other congregations, this may be their only opportunity to experience evangelical ministry.

The important thing, once again, is to approach this involvement with a positive attitude. We must encourage good people to become deanery synod representatives, and the clergy must make sure they attend meetings with them. Instead of being seen as a joke and a chore, the deanery should be seen as a 'mission field', where we once again seek the transformation of the Church as well as taking the opportunity for the proclamation of the gospel.

Case Study: a deanery church-growth task group

Several years ago, all the deaneries in the Diocese of Chelmsford were required to come up with a 'deanery vision'.

Such exercises have been undertaken before, and have generally resulted in little other than new mergers of parishes under fewer full-time clergy, so the initial reaction was a rather weary cynicism.

As part of their response, however, our own Parochial Church Councils submitted a proposal for a 'Deanery Church-Growth Task Group' which would suggest ways of increasing Sunday attendance.

The proposal was accepted by the deanery synod and, almost inevitably, one of our clergy was asked to chair the group. (It should be pointed out that gaining the confidence of the synod by regular attendance and participation was a necessary prelude to this request.)

As a result of the task group's efforts, church growth has been on the agenda of every deanery synod meeting for the past three years and has now become part of our collective 'ethos'. This has also provided an opportunity for the more evangelical parishes to share with others what they do and why they do it.

No one's interests are really served by keeping our congregations isolated from other Anglican churches in the same locality. And if we fear that the result of rubbing shoulders with them is that our own people will be 'corrupted' and led astray, perhaps we should have more confidence in them and in our pastoral abilities.

Securing the succession

Nevertheless, there is one area where it is vital to be careful about our own people, and that is when an incumbent moves on.

Sad to say, this is sometimes an occasion for diocesan officialdom to seek to alter the spiritual character of the parish, especially (it has to be said) if this is of a more conservative variety. In one situation of which I have personal knowledge, a very pleasant, but conservative, evangelical clergyman was replaced by a less conservative, but still evangelical, successor. He, however, was followed by an undoubted theological liberal who was particularly favoured by the local bishop. That appointment didn't work out, but the parish concerned is now in a very confused place.

If a minister has worked hard to build up an evangelical ministry, it is tragic if that is demolished by poor decisions regarding their replacement. It is therefore vital that before a minister moves on, the congregation and the Parochial Church Council are fully briefed on the process of finding a replacement.

In some situations, PCCs can be helped by 'patrons'. These derive from an ancient arrangement whereby certain individuals, or even bodies such as university colleges, have the right to 'present' candidates to serve in certain parishes, provided they meet with the approval of the bishop and the official 'parish representatives'. In many cases, the bishop is himself the patron and therefore this does not apply, but unfortunately bishops have taken to using their own legal powers to suspend the right of presentation, with the effect that the influence of the patron and the parish representatives is much diminished.

Bishops are generally only supposed to use this power when there are proposals for reorganizing the parish concerned (or affecting the vicarage), but they have often acted when there are no specific proposal in place and there may then be questions over the continuing 'tradition' of the parish. At some stage this practice ought to be subject to legal clarification, especially with the changes resulting from the introduction of 'common tenure'. In the meantime, thorough briefing and a strong will is needed.

Part of the difficulty, of course, is that PCC members usually have very little knowledge of ecclesiastical law and equally little experience of handling these sorts of situations, whereas bishops and archdeacons are very familiar with the legalities, even if they don't always adhere strictly to them. It may therefore be helpful to 'twin' vacant evangelical parishes with someone who can advise and encourage them, particularly if they do not have a patron in the position to do so.

For the more conservative evangelical parishes, who wish to stick to the earlier tradition of a 'male only' incumbent or priest-in-charge, it is also vital (and helpful) to pass both the available 'Resolutions' (A and B) under the existing Priests (Ordination of

Women) Measure.[49] Personally, I have long advised that they ought also to pass the so-called 'Resolution C', which is actually a petition, under the 1993 Episcopal Ministry Act of Synod, for provision of additional ministry by a bishop in sympathy with their position.[50] This makes a great deal of difference if the bishop with legal responsibility is over-reaching himself with regards to the parish tradition.

Similarly for conservative evangelical parishes, when and if the new legislation comes in regarding women bishops, they must use every provision available.

Meanwhile, even the broader evangelical parishes must not be complacent. It is a sad fact that such advice is necessary, but the truth is that we are in a struggle for the Church, where some of those in charge either do not understand or do not agree with the theological principles and practices this entails.

Working with the diocese

Having said all the above, however, if we are going to transform the denomination, we must stop habitually treating diocesan officialdom as 'the enemy'.

This may be difficult! Certainly one can find all sorts of problems at this level, including political machinations, arrogance and incompetence. There is no excuse for such things. However, an attitude of habitual hostility is both unproductive and unlikely to lead to denominational transformation. On the contrary, we need to start appreciating the presence of and need for thoroughly converted and godly people within the managerial bodies of the Church, who understand and are in sympathy with its proper evangelistic aims. (Moreover, a positive attitude towards and engagement with the local diocese is itself something of a protection for ourselves.)

Those of us who are fortunate enough to deploy parish

---

[49] See http://www.legislation.gov.uk/ukcm/1993/2/schedule/1

[50] See http://www.ebbsfleet.org.uk/actofsynod93.htm

administrators know how much they matter. Indeed, it is surely significant that when the early Church recognized the need for administrative specialists, they chose not those whom they couldn't use for anything else but some of their best: "men ... known to be full of the Spirit and wisdom" (Acts 6:3). Given what happened subsequently, we may argue they were over-qualified.[51] Nevertheless, the point is made that 'admin' is not something you should palm off to the 'unspiritual'.

We therefore need to show, where possible, our appreciation of those who work in these structures, to pray for them and to cooperate with them as much as we can. We also need to look out for vacancies and, when they occur, to encourage good candidates to apply for the posts on the grounds that they represent a vital ministry.

The issue of non-parochial diocesan clergy can be more problematic. Understandably, but unfortunately, institutions tend to take on people in these posts who will 'fit in'. Given that the prevailing ethos of most dioceses is a 'middle-of-the-road inclusivism', bishops' staffs, training officers, selectors, rural and area deans and the like tend to be of a similar type.[52] The result is a theological blandness (with a bias to liberalism) which makes it quite difficult to support and endorse diocesan gatherings, official conferences, study-days, courses and so on. Moreover, it can be difficult to break into 'the system' if you present with a theologically-conservative outlook or reputation.

Nevertheless, we do not automatically have to operate in opposition, even if we cannot support with enthusiasm. One alternative is to offer events or initiatives which come from an evangelical stable, but which are made available to the diocese as a whole.

---

[51] One was martyred for his preaching and another went on to be a pioneering evangelist.

[52] L J Francis, M Robbins, K Kaldor and K Castle, 'Psychological Type and Work-related Psychological Health Among Clergy in Australia, England and New Zealand' (*Journal of Psychology and Christianity*, October 2009). This study supported previous findings that in Myers-Briggs terms, Anglican clergy in general are of a similar type, preferring "introversion over extraversion, sensing over intuition, feeling over thinking and judging over perceiving".

Case Study: a diocesan bible conference

In the closing years of the 1990s I was at a committee meeting of the Chelmsford Diocesan Evangelical Association where people were praising the management of a recent diocesan conference for the laity but lamenting the content.

"Why don't we organize something ourselves?" I said., "Something that would deliver what we wanted, but at a diocesan level."

Inevitably I got the job, but the CDEA agreed to provide the initial funding. The idea was to start a series of annual Bible-teaching conferences that would extend over ten years, with the aim of 'putting good biblical teaching at the heart of the diocese'.

A large organizing committee, representing a diversity of views, was set up and the concept was canvassed at a series of breakfast meetings around the diocese to which local evangelical clergy were invited to hear a presentation and to give their opinion.

After establishing that there was sufficient interest and support, a date and speaker were booked for early 2000. However, to make the point that this was for the whole diocese, the venue selected was the cathedral and the diocesan bishop was invited to launch the event.

Attendance was enormously encouraging, with over 200 coming from across the diocese, and although the venue presented considerable difficulties by way of facilities and timing, we were encouraged enough to go ahead with planning the next year.

Then the problems began. The cost of equipping the cathedral was so high that we were grateful to find an alternative, and functionally more suitable, venue in the Central Baptist Church. However, this took us away from the physical heart of the diocese.

We also began to lose people from the organizing committee and although this meant that meeting together became easier, it was evident that the theological 'profile' was becoming more conservative. This in turn, however, led to the withdrawal of support from other evangelicals who felt that we were not sufficiently broad. Indeed there were rumours that the Conference was all some kind of political 'plot'.

Attendance began to drop and discouragement affected the remaining organizers — by now just three. Had we not had the support of one of the large churches in the diocese, no doubt the project would have folded.

Nevertheless, we persevered and for the seventh conference we acquired the services of a new administrator, once again illustrating the importance of good administrative staff. Numbers began to pick up, we received regular support from one of our Area bishops and in 2010 the newly-appointed diocesan bishop, Stephen Cottrell, attended the event even though he was not yet in post.

In important ways, therefore, we feel that we have gained the support and recognition of the diocese. Nevertheless, we believe it is crucial to maintain 'quality control' over the speakers, who have all been, and will continue to be, theologically conservative and evangelical.

It has been hard work, but after ten years we have decided to carry on, and we do indeed believe we are beginning to see the fulfilment of the original vision (and we have paid back the loan to the CDEA).

Two important principles must, however, be maintained if such initiatives are going to promote the transformation of the Church. The first is that they must be presented positively, as contributions to diocesan life, not as competing attractions. Secondly, however, we must strictly maintain the quality of what we ourselves offer. If we aim at the normal notion of theological 'balance', or if we compromise on content, what we offer will not be capable of transformation — we will simply have 'gone along' with what already happens.

Additionally, we should always seek out and reinforce what is good, even if it is not as good as we might hope. We can and should, for example, support everything the diocese does which either is itself a positive thing or which offers an opportunity for positive involvement, especially in teaching. We should involve ourselves in these things as much as possible and encourage anything which is a 'step in the right direction'.

Even when dealing with desperate problems within the congregations he addressed, the Apostle Paul never entirely dropped his tone of tenderness and concern for them. The Galatians may have been "foolish" (Gal 3:1), but they were still addressed as "my children" (4:19). In the same way, therefore, a prophetic engagement with the Church does not require us to treat all those who are in error with hostility or contempt.

Certainly we must be firm in confronting false teachers (1 Timothy 1:3), but we must treat the Church of Christ as a whole with the same regard that he has for it himself — willing to rebuke, but wanting to redeem. The crucial thing is to maintain an open stance towards the diocese, even whilst one may rightly wish to be critical. We must rigorously maintain our own theological standards — this is not about accepting the 'middle of the road' ethos as the right one. But we must look to share with others at every opportunity rather than to quarantine ourselves and our people from the institution.

Appreciating the episcopate

Back in 1986 when he spoke at the Evangelical Ministry Assembly, Phillip Jensen came out with the classic line, "Bishops are deacons and priests are bishops." It was a brilliant, yet in some ways unfortunate, observation. On the one hand, much of a modern bishop's work is actually 'diaconal' — the modern equivalent of "waiting on tables" (Acts 6:2) via committees and administration, rather than giving their energies to "prayer and the ministry of the word" (6:4).[53] Far too many bishops spend far too little time on what even they believe ought to be their chief functions.

What those of us who were at the 1986 Assembly heard, though, was not that bishops should change their priorities but that they don't really matter much anyway. And that is a misleading, and ultimately unhelpful, attitude to adopt when you are part of an episcopal church.

Ironically, anyone familiar with the history of the diocese of Sydney, from which Phillip comes, will know that its own bishops have mattered enormously, from the appointment of Howard Mowll to that of the present incumbent, Phillip's brother Peter.

Phillip stated very strongly at the time that "bishops are not the answer", and insofar as generals are not 'the answer' to winning battles or managers 'the answer' to making a profit, I would have to agree with him. But bishops who, as Samson Mwaluda observed, take seriously their calling to be the "vision bearing evangelist-teachers", setting the right tone for their dioceses in terms of mission and ministry, can make a vast difference. Anyone who doubts this need only look at the current focus on mission in the Sydney diocese.

For better or for worse, what the bishop cares about is what the diocese will recognize as important. Unfortunately, that is just as true if he cares about the wrong things as when he cares about the right things. Sadly, very few bishops of my personal acquaintance have conveyed that they care about truth and salvation as much as they care about order and administration. Consequently, most of my experience of diocesan life has been something of a disappointment. Nevertheless, many of us still look back wistfully to J C Ryle of Liverpool or overseas to men like Greg Venables, formerly of the

---

[53] The title 'Archdeacon' has the merit of being almost entirely accurate, since the job is virtually all administration. The problem in terms of the Church hierarchy is that you don't really need to be theologically trained to carry it out (though you should certainly be godly, as I have argued).

Southern Cone, or Mwaluda himself.

What we need is the conviction that it could happen here!

It is wrong to say, as some do, that the ministry of diocesan clergy flows from the bishop. It flows from Christ. But the bishop is the gate-keeper for ministry in the diocese. He can make crucial appointments, especially when it comes to suffragans and archdeacons. In many cases he is the patron of a substantial number of parishes, meaning he has a significant say in the clergy who will work there. And by exercising his right of suspending presentation to a benefice, he can have even more influence.

The bishop is entitled (indeed he is required) to ask questions of those being ordained or licensed by himself. It is his job to make sure that they are themselves faithful to the gospel and equipped for the task. The bishop is also the voice of the Church. What the bishop says is perceived as what the Church stands for — and the bishop also has public opportunities way beyond those of typical parish clergy. Not only is this a matter of pronouncing on the affairs of the day. It provides a backdrop against which ordinary clergy and parishioners can speak about the things of the gospel in their own contexts, where what the bishop has said can be a help or a hindrance.

So despite what some bishops say about their 'limited powers', they have unparalleled opportunities to affect the ministry of the Church.

Arguably, then, the problem with the episcopate is not only that some evangelicals don't take it seriously but that many *bishops* don't take it seriously. They may be conscientious regarding the duties imposed on them by the agenda of the institution. But this is not that same as the agenda conceived in 1945 — the conversion of England and the transformation of the Church into a vehicle for evangelism.

Sadly, this is frequently true even of those from an evangelical background. Far too many of them seem to regard the issues that once concerned them in parish life as irrelevant once they have achieved higher office. As a Puritan, Lord Burghley, put it over four hundred years ago,

> I see such worldliness in many that were otherwise affected before they came to cathedral chairs, that I fear the places alter the men.[54]

Of course, the bishop must be a bishop to 'the whole diocese', but this ought to mean ensuring that everyone and everywhere in the diocese receives a sound, gospel-centred ministry capable (at the very least) of bringing about the conversion of those who do not yet know Christ. Certainly a bishop who jealously guarded his own pulpit when he was a parish priest ought to do the same for the pulpits of his diocese. Anything less than that is a dereliction of duty.

An interesting comparison with the Anglican attitude can be made with the Church of Rome, where bishops make five-yearly 'visitations' to parishes, either in person or by proxy. The instructions make challenging reading:

> The pastoral visit is one of the ways ... through which the Bishop maintains personal contact with the clergy and with other members of the People of God. It is an occasion to rejuvenate the energies of those engaged in evangelization, to praise, encourage and reassure them. It is also an opportunity to invite the faithful to a renewal of Christian life and to an ever more intense apostolic activity.[55]

Would that more Anglican bishops saw their rôle this way! Yet too often, bishops are averse to criticism and resistant to change. Richard Hooker, a staunch supporter of episcopacy, had some cogent points to make in this regard:

> Wherefore lest bishops forget themselves, as if none on earth had authority to touch their states, let them continually bear in mind, that it is rather the force of custom, whereby the Church having so long found it good to continue under the regiment of her virtuous bishops, doth still uphold, maintain, and honour them in that respect, than that any such true and heavenly law can be shewed, by the evidence whereof it may of a truth appear that the Lord himself hath appointed

---

[54] Quoted in Patrick Collinson, *The Elizabethan Puritan Movement*, (London: Jonathan Cape, 1967) 49.

[55] Directory for the Pastoral Ministry of Bishops, III. The Pastoral Visit, 220, 'The Nature of the Pastoral Visit', http://www.vatican.va/roman_curia/congregations/cbishops/documents/rc_con_cbishops_doc_20040222_apostolorum-successores_en.html. retrieved 24 August 2011.

> presbyters for ever to be under the regiment of bishops, in what sort soever they behave themselves. Let this consideration be a bridle unto them, let it teach them not to disdain the advice of their presbyters, but to use their authority with so much the greater humility and moderation, as a sword which the Church hath power to take from them.[56]

We must also caution those who seem to rally to the bishop 'right or wrong' when such criticisms are voiced. It is not a part of any biblical (and therefore Anglican) ecclesiology, to respect an office-holder who fails to uphold the gospel or to be faithful to his (or indeed her) office. Too often we are presented with a false dichotomy: do you accept the office of the bishop or do you expect him to believe the same things as you do? When it comes to the *fundamentals* of the faith, however, all Anglicans should surely believe the same things. Episcopal office does not excuse one from this! On the contrary, it puts one in the front line of contending for the faith.[57]

Previous generations of evangelicals could hardly be accused of giving too much respect to the episcopal office. The result, however, has been either to abandon the episcopate to those with less-than-clear doctrines and aims, or to abandon evangelical brethren when they have become bishops, rather than upholding them in their new rôle and calling them to account in the way that Hooker envisages above.

Evangelicals ought to be at the forefront of encouraging episcopal ministry and even, where opportunity presents, taking it on themselves. They can, and should, back the bishop and tell him of their support, for example, when he does something positive. After all, if they find themselves appointed to this office they will need all the help they can get to withstand the pressures to

---

[56] *Laws of Ecclesiastical Polity*, VII.v.8

[57] In the Prayer Book Ordinal, the priest being consecrated as bishop is asked, "Be you ready, with all faithful diligence, to banish and drive away all erroneous and strange doctrine contrary to God's Word; and both privately and openly to call upon and encourage others to the same?" The bishop is not just to preach the truth but to have a word in private with those who do not.

compromise and the brickbats that will come at them from within and without the Church if they are faithful to Christ's calling.

Our satisfaction should lie, however, not in the mere fact that evangelicals are being made bishops, as if this were some kind of institutional 'prize', but in evangelical bishops using their office to promote the mission of the Church and the conversion of England. Only then will it really be worth their being appointed in the first place.

Revising the appointments process

There are some aspects of episcopacy in the Church of England, however, which certainly call for reform, and one of them is the way in which bishops are appointed.

The arcane nature of the appointments process regarding diocesan bishops is comprehensively described (and debunked) by Colin Buchanan in his *Cut the Connection*.[58] The only significant change since he wrote in 1994 is that the Crown Appointments Commission is now the Crown Nominations Commission and that the Prime Minister now only receives one name from the the latter body rather than the two he used to receive from the former.

Apart from that, things are essentially unchanged from the system put in place in 1977 under the then-prime minister Jim Callaghan. It is still the case that the monarch notionally makes the final choice. It is still the case that the monarch sends a license (the *congé d'élire*) to the dean or provost of the cathedral of the vacant see authorising him or her to convene a chapter meeting where they pray for the guidance of the Holy Spirit to elect a new bishop. And it is still the case that, by the same post, the monarch sends 'letters missive' telling them the name of the person to elect!

This is all quite fun, in the same way that it is fun seeing Black Rod knocking three times on the door of the House of Commons

---

[58] Colin Buchanan, *Cut the Connection: disestablishment and the Church of England* (London: Darton Longman & Todd, 1994) 81-104.

before he is let in (no one ever calls out, "Who is it?"). But Buchanan is surely right in saying that the appointment of bishops could do with an overhaul.

In fact, just such an overhaul has been considered, in a report by a committee chaired by Baroness Perry, titled *Working with the Spirit: choosing diocesan bishops - a review of the operation of the Crown Appointments Commission and related matters.*[59]

Unfortunately, the Perry Report rejected any notion of truly radical change, even whilst it recognized the existence of genuine problems:

> The submissions we received indicated that there was no general demand to change the overall shape of the system, nor have we identified any need to do so. At the same time, we received evidence of widespread unease about important aspects of how the system operates.[60]

Amongst these problems was noted the "excessive secrecy" surrounding the process. (Members of the CNC are not allowed to tell even spouses where they are meeting, and the whole discussion process is meant to be strictly confidential, particularly as to which names are being considered.)

Moreover, there might be added the fact that the make-up of the CNC means the same few people are repeatedly involved in the selection of diocesan bishops, giving them enormous influence over the character of the Church which results from these appointments.

Thus despite seeing "no need" for fundamental change, the report went on to note that,

> [...] we were unable to conclude from the evidence submitted to us that there is a general confidence that the way the system for choosing our diocesan bishops works is demonstrably fair, robust and effective.[61]

---

[59] The Archbishops' Council of the Church of England, *Working with the Spirit: choosing diocesan bishops — a review of the operation of the Crown Appointments Commission and related matters* (London: Church House Publishing, 2001).

[60] *Ibid.* 85.

[61] *Ibid.* 86

Now this is surely an extraordinary admission. Furthermore, as we have noted already, there is an acknowledged bias in the process of senior appointments, not least when it comes to the more-conservative theological elements in the Church.[62] Indeed, the Perry Report itself gives figures which suggest a distinct bias against such candidates.[63]

> The figures for the last five years have given rise, in some quarters at least, to a perception of unfairness towards those who are perceived as traditional catholics and a suspicion that the CAC [Crown Appointments Commission] has not acted in the spirit of the Act of Synod.[64]

This 'suspicion' was unfortunately shown to be justified when, in 2011, the diocesan 'Statement of Needs' drawn up for the appointment of the new Bishop of Salisbury specifically excluded anyone who would not be prepared to ordain women, in direct contradiction to the 1993 Episcopal Ministry Act of Synod.

Nevertheless, despite any resentments or disappointments they may feel, evangelicals must think positively about what is best for the Church of England, not what 'safeguards' their own position.

More telling than the Perry Report's admissions about bias against the more-conservative candidates was what it had to say about the tendency, particularly evident at the time, to appoint as diocesan bishops those who were already suffragans (ie, assistant bishops in a diocese):

> It has been suggested to us in evidence that those chosen to be suffragan bishops are often 'safe choices' rather than people likely to cause trouble, reliable pastors rather than impressive thinkers or prophets, or (to use an analogy from the business world) good managers rather than directors who view things from a much wider perspective, team players rather than team leaders.[65]

---

[62] See p19 above.

[63] *Op cit*, 26.

[64] *Ib id*, 27.

[65] *Ibid*. 17.

This may seem a bit harsh on suffragan bishops who, after all, are just doing their best. And some have made excellent diocesans. Overall, however, it *has* sometimes felt as if the Church of England were indeed made up of 'the bland leading the blind'.

Here is not the place to go into detailed suggestions of just how the system might be reformed, though surely there is room for greater openness and wider democratic involvement. The Perry Report specifically rejected the idea of open elections, but there is surely no *a priori* reason why the choice of a diocesan bishop should not involve more than a handful of members of the diocese.

Meanwhile, the system *has* improved. Vacancies in see are now notified in the Church press and people are invited to submit names. Nevertheless, there is still a tight control over the appointments process and a sense that it involves 'jobs for the favoured boys' — and soon to be, girls.

A suffragan bishop of my acquaintance once remarked to a gathered group of evangelical clergy that, despite the increasing numbers of evangelicals at every level of the Church, the atmosphere in the 'corridors of power' remained resolutely liberal-catholic. While this is the case, there is surely room to question the appropriateness of a system of appointments which seems to favour the perpetuation of a self-selecting oligarchy.

Re-forming our theology

Hopefully it will be clear by now that we cannot be content with an 'enclave' approach, whereby we simply create a 'space' for evangelicals within a wider, and ever more diverse, Church of England. That has been the mistake of too many evangelicals in the past and the present and applies equally to both open evangelicals and conservatives. As has been observed already, the 'open' error is to embrace too much diversity, the 'conservative' error is to give up on the institution.

Nor are we simply 'affirming' every outlook and attitude within the wider Church. As we observed at the outset, *Towards the Conversion of England* did not present evangelism as an 'option' for some. Rather, personal evangelism was envisaged as the proper task of the whole Church. But that would also have required, to some extent, a shared core theology — one that assumed, for example, the reality of and necessity for conversion, that presented Christ as Saviour and King, that saw the Church as a distinct body of believers with a message for a world lost in sin and in need of salvation, and so on.

Perhaps it was this challenge that was really too great for the post-war leadership of the Church. We may never know. At present, however, it is clearly the case that theological diversity is quite deliberately encouraged as a matter of course within the Church of England.

Yet with this diversity in belief comes uncertainty in mission. In 1995, for example, the Doctrine Commission published a report titled *The Mystery of Salvation*, which began by discussing the 'clear and present danger' of people in a house fire or on a sinking ship:

> ... if we are to speak of salvation in a Christian sense we have also to seek more clarity about the peril in which the world is believed to stand.[66]

Yet by the end of the report, that peril was still a mystery!

Conversion requires a theology, both from the one proclaiming the message and from the one receiving it. It is not a very complicated theology, but it is nevertheless quite specific. Thus in Acts 2, we read the first ever Christian evangelistic talk, and it concludes with this appeal from the Apostle Peter,

> "Therefore let all Israel be assured of this: God has made this Jesus, whom you crucified, both Lord and Christ."
>
> When the people heard this, they were cut to the heart and said to Peter and the other apostles, "Brothers, what shall we do?"

---

[66] Church of England, *The Mystery of Salvation: The Story of God's Gift — a Report by the Doctrine Commission of the Church of England* (London: Church House Publishing, 1995), 1.

> Peter replied, "Repent and be baptized, every one of you, in the
> name of Jesus Christ for the forgiveness of your sins. And you will
> receive the gift of the Holy Spirit." (Acts 2:36-38)

The key elements of the gospel here are these: sin that separates us from God, Jesus who is Lord and Christ (ie Saviour), repentance wherein we are reconciled to God, baptism which unites us to Christ and makes us members of the Church, and the gift of the Holy Spirit whereby we walk in newness of life. You might think such a basic and foundational presentation of the Church's message would be held in common by all. Yet in reality this is just one of many theologies of salvation within the Church of England.[67]

And this is of crucial important, for our theology in other areas depends precisely on our soteriology — our doctrine of salvation. Thus the Apostle Paul sums up his message in these words to the Corinthians:

> For what I received I passed on to you as of first importance: that
> Christ died for our sins according to the Scriptures, that he was
> buried, that he was raised on the third day according to the
> Scriptures ... (1 Cor 15:3-4)

All our major theological themes can be developed from this starting point: who Christ is and why he died for our sins, what this achieved and how, who we are that Christ should die for us, why he was raised from death and what difference this makes — bearing in mind all the time that these things are to be understood "according to the Scriptures".

Yet depending largely on the minister in charge, you could go into a dozen different Anglican churches and find a dozen different permutations and variations to these and other fundamental

---

[67] Rowan Williams, for example, sees the message in the early part of Acts as being peculiar only to those people who actually put Jesus on trial. When Peter says to the Sanhedrin, "Salvation is found in no one else, for there is no other name under heaven given to men by which we must be saved" (Acts 4:12), that is only true of *them*. For other people, 'salvation' may be found in other names. (See Rowan Williams, *Resurrection: Interpreting the Easter Gospel*, [London: Darton Longman & Todd, 2002], 3-5: "... once it is established that the persecuted Church 'embodies' Jesus as victim, the definition of the oppressor, the identity of the condemning court, becomes ever wider. [...] it is a gospel for all.")

questions.

Some will be virtual Roman Catholics, even using the Missal in preference to official services. Others will be covert Baptists. You will find old-fashioned Arminians in one place and Calvinists in another, and in yet other places those with no regard for traditional or conventional understandings of God whatsoever. One bishop will happily redefine the Holy Spirit as 'She', another will reject the Reformation understandings of salvation and redemption. As to the Bible, it may be regarded as anything from the inerrant word of God to a document at least some of which deserves to be consigned to the flames.[68]

The outside observer might be forgiven for thinking that the basic principle of the Church of England (as one archdeacon observed ruefully in my hearing) is that, "We don't mind what you believe, so long as you keep the institutional rules." To put it another way, we seem to be back in the days of the Judges when, "Everyone did what was right in his own eyes" (Judg 21:25).

Yet in fact the Church of England does have doctrinal boundaries, it's just that we seem to have forgotten them. Thus the Church's 'Canons' — its official regulations — state that,

> The doctrine of the Church of England is grounded in the Holy Scriptures, and in such teachings of the ancient Fathers and Councils of the Church as are agreeable to the said Scriptures. In particular such doctrine is to be found in the Thirty-nine Articles of Religion, *The Book of Common Prayer*, and the Ordinal.[69]

Notice, once again, the prior commitment of the Church of England is to Scripture. However, the Articles, the Prayer Book and the Ordinal are all described as agreeable to the Word of God (see also Canons A2, A3 and A4).[70] And although there may be room

---

[68] Admittedly the latter actually happened in the Church in Wales, but doubtless there are those clergy in England who would sympathize. In credit to him, the local bishop did at least rebuke the actions of the clergyman concerned.

[69] Canon A5, 'Of the doctrine of the Church of England'.

[70] Notice, incidentally, that the wording of these Canons also has a bearing on how we should regard Scripture (assuming that is what is indicated by the phrase 'the Word of God').

amongst the wider community of Christian believers for other interpretations of the Bible, for example on the practice of infant baptism, the Church of England through its 'formularies' declares that its collective mind is made up on certain issues.

It ought also to be remembered that the foundations of the English Reformation included an 'Act of Uniformity', designed to introduce one single, unifying, liturgy: a *Book of COMMON Prayer*. Many people are rightly impressed by the rhythmic beauty of Prayer Book English, but its importance goes much deeper than that. As the Bishop of Chelmsford, Stephen Cottrell, recently observed,

> The Church of England has always believed that we learn and express our doctrine through our worship. The *Book of Common Prayer*, therefore, does not just contain beautiful liturgy, it is the finest expression of what we believe.[71]

It is often alleged that the 'spirit' of Anglicanism is one of compromise, but this was certainly not the case during the Reformation. Rather, the spirit then was an uncompromising "reducing of the people to a most perfect and godly living, without error or superstition".[72]

The problem, though, is how to apply Canon A5 in practice. On the one hand, some people see the formularies as relevant only to a particular time in history — as merely representing what the Church once believed, not what anyone actually needs to believe today. On the other hand, there are those who argue that unless you agree to the letter with absolutely *everything* stated in the Articles yourself, you cannot demand that anyone else agrees with *anything* they state. Some go on to say that everyone therefore ought to believe them entirely and without question (and indeed that is how they were originally intended), others say that since this would clearly be absurd, we are back to the position that they are merely of historical interest.

---

[71] http://www.bcp350.org.uk/supporters.php retrieved 22 August 2011.

[72] Cranmer's Preface 'Of Ceremonies: Why some be abolished, and some retained'.

In trying to find a balance, however, we may note that the content of the formularies is not all of equal significance. Article XXXIX, for example, states that,

> ... Christian religion doth not prohibit but that a man may swear when the magistrate requireth in a cause of faith and charity ...

Some Christians would disagree, quoting in support Matthew 5:34, "But I tell you, do not swear at all." However, it is clearly not a 'salvation' issue and, even as a social issue, today is of minor importance.[73] Indeed, even Anglican clergy are allowed by Canon to *affirm* the Oath of Allegiance in their licensing, rather than swear it.[74]

On the other hand, Article II, for example, touches on matters central to faith and salvation:

> ... Christ ... truly suffered, was crucified, dead and buried, to reconcile his Father to us, and to be a sacrifice, not only for original guilt, but also for all actual sins of men.

A much more serious discussion ought to ensue if any member of the clergy denied that this were true. The Articles can thus be arranged in a kind of 'hierarchy' of significance. But so too, therefore, can disputes about or disagreements with the Articles. It is a minor concern if someone questions whether General Councils "may not be gathered together without the commandment and will of Princes" (Article XXI). But we should surely be very worried if someone doubts that "Christ did truly rise again from death" (Article IV).

The real problem when it comes to the Articles and the Prayer Book, however, is not that we regularly face an 'all or nothing' choice but that they hardly get a look-in when it comes to Anglican practice.

Take, for example, the long-running dispute about the theology of justification held by N T Wright, a prominent academic and

---

[73] By and large, for example, radical Christians no longer use it to call into question the authority of the state.

[74] Canon C.13.3.

former Bishop of Durham.

Wright has been questioned by numerous evangelical scholars, and supported by some others. Wright has issued clarifications and others have issued further comments. Almost no one, however, seems to have asked whether what Wright suggests accords with Article XI, 'Of Justification':

> We are accounted righteous before God, only for the merit of our Lord and Saviour Jesus Christ by Faith, and not for our own works or deservings: Wherefore, that we are justified by Faith only is a most wholesome Doctrine, and very full of comfort ...

If it could be stated categorically by Wright himself that his position agrees with the Articles, this ought to set a number of troubled Anglican hearts at rest. This is not to say that Wright's position necessarily is at odds with the Articles. Nor, if it is not, does this mean we shut down the debate. It is, however, to suggest that a renewed awareness of and engagement with the Anglican formularies would radically change the way that the Church of England approaches the task of doing theology.

The argument here is not for an unquestioning imposition of the theology of the Articles, the Prayer Book or the Ordinal — any more than Canon A5 requires an unquestioning acceptance of the teachings of the ancient Fathers or the rulings of the early Church Councils. Scripture ought to be our final authority, and the Articles themselves make even the Creeds subordinate to what the Bible says. But the formularies provide a grid through which Scripture is read and understood, and this ought to set the boundaries regarding the way we do our theology. As Dr Jim Packer once put it, the Church of England is not supposed to be 'a kind of Noah's ark' in which any and every shade of opinion finds a shelter.

Every minister at his or her ordination or appointment to a new parish makes what is called the Declaration of Assent. First, the following statement is read out:

> The Church of England is part of the One, Holy, Catholic and Apostolic Church worshipping the one true God, Father, Son and Holy Spirit. It professes the faith uniquely revealed in the Holy

Scriptures and set forth in the catholic creeds, which faith the Church is called upon to proclaim afresh in each generation. Led by the Holy Spirit, it has borne witness to Christian truth in its historic formularies, the Thirty-nine Articles of Religion, the Book of Common Prayer and the Ordering of Bishops, Priests and Deacons. In the declaration you are about to make will you affirm your loyalty to this inheritance of faith as your inspiration and guidance under God in bringing the grace and truth of Christ to this generation and making Him known to those in your care?

Then the minister replies,

I A B, do so affirm, and accordingly declare my belief in the faith which is revealed in the Holy Scriptures and set forth in the catholic creeds and to which the historic formularies of the Church of England bear witness; and in public prayer and administration of the sacraments, I will use only the forms of service which are authorised or allowed by Canon.

Such a solemn declaration ought to mean more than, "I know what the Church of England once said it believed, but I personally believe whatever it is I choose to believe." After all, the statement about using services "authorized or allowed by Canon" is supposed to be taken seriously — why not the declaration about "my belief"?

Making sense of this is actually an enormous challenge for the Church of England, but evangelicals should have least to fear and most to gain from the process. Ultimately, however, this is not about the triumph of one theological position over another but about upholding the theology necessary to the conversion of England. This is not a matter of finding a compromise viewpoint that holds us all together and 'gets the job done'. Rather, it is about the most basic issues underlying the fundamentals of the Christian faith.

I am pleased to note that, when it comes to 'The Doctrine of the Church of England', the book by Martin Davie which I referred to rather negatively earlier, appeals to the formularies in general and the Articles in particular.[75] Although I don't always agree with his interpretation and application, it does demonstrate that these historic statements of faith are, as he says, "not seen simply as historic

---

[75] Davie, Martin. *A guide to the Church of England* (London: Mowbray, 2008), 80-106.

statements of doctrine".[76] Rather, they are to be viewed "dynamically", as a constant source of (in the words of the Declaration of Assent) "inspiration and guidance".

Disciplining ourselves

If we agree that there ought to be a minimum standard of Anglican doctrine, we ought also to realize that certain standards should apply to evangelicals themselves. Yet 'evangelicalism' is notoriously hard to define, as witnessed by the perennial supply of books and essays with titles like 'What is an Evangelical?'.[77]

A further issue for Anglican evangelicals is that there are evangelicals who are *not* Anglicans. We may agree with them on some things but disagree on others, such as infant baptism or the rôle of free will. When I was a university chaplain, I even found myself working reasonably comfortably with Strict Brethren and Seventh Day Adventists. We got along, but clearly we could not have formed a denomination between us!

We have to make sense of our unity with those outside Anglicanism as well as our membership of the Church of England. Yet that experience of unity does demonstrate an important point. There is *something* about evangelicalism which evokes a sense of mutual recognition, even when we can find many subjects on which to disagree (such as the observation of the Sabbath or the wearing of head-coverings in the congregation).

Many different features have been invoked to explain this. Often people will point to the 'evangelical' attitude to the Bible. But even here there is room for disagreement! Some evangelicals are 'inerrantists', happy to sign up to precise definitions such as the *Chicago Statement* which runs to nineteen 'Articles', plus a Preface and Exposition.[78] Others would be less inclined to such an exact

---

[76] *Ibid.* 83.

[77] In 1971, Dr Martyn Lloyd-Jones published a book with just this title. More recently, Mark Thompson of Moore Theological College tackled the same issue in his booklet *Saving the Heart*, subtitled *What is an Evangelical?*

definition.

The key to the evangelical identity, however, surely lies in the label itself. It is a particular understanding of the gospel — the *evangel* — which creates and sustains the common bond evangelicals share with one another.

Paul's summary in 1 Corinthians 15:3-4 identifies the core *content* of the gospel as being that "Christ died for our sins according to the Scriptures, that he was buried, that he was raised on the third day according to the Scriptures". Yet non-evangelicals would also claim agreement with that statement. Since the Reformation, therefore, the defining evangelical conviction has been that faith in this message is both *necessary to* and *sufficient for* entering into a right relationship with God and receiving all his promised blessings, beginning with the Spirit who is "a deposit, guaranteeing what is to come" (2 Cor 1:22).

It is these three convictions, regarding the nature, the necessity and the sufficiency of the gospel, that are at the heart of evangelical identity. They are also fundamental to the work of conversion, however, and therefore arguably they are fundamental to the nature of the Church. Furthermore, they can each be found expressed in the Anglican formularies.

Yet there are many other points of possible disagreement amongst Christians generally which are ultimately of less significance. One of the necessary features of 'denominationalism' is that it establishes institutional parameters within which people can work on the basis of agreement about some of these disputed issues (such as baptism) whilst not denying the genuineness of the faith of others and their relationship with God.

The real problem amongst evangelicals comes when people depart from the understanding they had of the gospel when they were converted.

In presenting his outline of the gospel, the Apostle Paul warns specifically against this:

---

[78] An internet search will identify numerous websites carrying the *Statement*.

> Now, brothers, I want to remind you of the gospel I preached to you,
> which you received and on which you have taken your stand. By this
> gospel you are saved, if you hold firmly to the word I preached to
> you. Otherwise, you have believed in vain. For what I received I
> passed on to you as of first importance: that Christ died for our sins
> according to the Scriptures ... (1 Cor 15:1-3)

And in other parts of the Scriptures we find warnings against departing from "the faith that was once for all entrusted to the saints" (Jude 3). Of course, faith may grow and mature and in that way it will differ from our earlier 'faith' — this itself ought to be a gospel principle, since the gospel brings us into a living, and therefore developing, encounter with God:

> We have much to say about this, but it is hard to explain because
> you are slow to learn. In fact, though by this time you ought to be
> teachers, you need someone to teach you the elementary truths of
> God's word all over again. You need milk, not solid food! (Heb
> 5:11-12)

But true Christian maturity is about expanding and developing our understanding and application of the *same principles* which were at the basis of our conversion, not wandering off after different, and contradictory, teachings. Hence Paul warned the churches in Galatia,

> ... even if we or an angel from heaven should preach a gospel other
> than the one we preached to you, let him be eternally condemned!
> (Gal 1:8)

The sad truth, however, is that many evangelicals indeed wander away from the gospel. Suppose you could go back in time and meet 'you' before you became a Christian. Given the opportunity, would 'you from the future' still witness to 'you from the past' so that you would still be converted by you? If the answer is 'no' then clearly your understanding of the gospel has changed. And if that is the case, you need to ask yourself some very serious questions!

Furthermore, in their book *The Churching of America, 1776-1990*, sociologists Roger Finke and Rodney Stark give repeated examples of how previously-growing denominations began to decline when liberalism took hold in the institutions, especially in the theological colleges, but also in the administration. People 'in the pews' lost confidence in their clergy and their leaders, whilst the clergy lost interest in evangelistic growth.

Theological 'traditionalism' is arguably therefore not just a matter of loyalty to the past but of effectiveness regarding proclaiming salvation in the present. Yet today in the Church of England, far too many people are holding onto the label 'evangelical' who would not evangelize anyone in the way that got them converted. Some of them have responsibility in evangelical parishes and organizations, yet in practical terms they are not evangelicals at all. The fact that this is the case means that we have to exercise a godly discipline amongst evangelicals.

We spoke earlier of the need to secure our parishes through the faithful ministry of the word of God. Yet the same is true of our organizations. And for specifically *Anglican* evangelicals, this suggests three lines of enquiry that ought to be followed when we make appointments.

The first is to check out someone's general grasp of the outlines of Anglican theology. Anyone and everyone responsible for making appointments, whether this is the bishops, members of interviewing panels, parish representatives, and so on, ought to ask some questions about the Creeds, the sacraments and the Articles.[79]

And then we should ask our specifically evangelical questions — questions designed to show how someone actually understands and applies the gospel. We could do worse than begin with a variation on the old 'Evangelism Explosion' doorstep poser:

> If Christ were to return today, what reason would you give him why

---

[79] Some evangelicals may be surprised to see the sacraments mentioned here. First, we should observe that the Church of England does recognize the sacraments. Secondly, we should observe it recognizes only two "Sacraments of the Gospel", the other practices "commonly called Sacraments ... being such as have grown partly of the corrupt following of the Apostles, partly are states of life allowed in the Scriptures" (Article XXV). Thirdly, it does have a theology of the gospel Sacraments, regarding what they are and why we practice them. Questions and answers in these areas will give a good indication of where someone stands on a number of issues.

he should welcome you into his kingdom?[80]

As the Australian evangelist John Chapman dryly observes, any answer that begins "Because I ..." is the wrong answer! But there are many other wrong answers available. What we say about our relationship with God and what this suggests Christ has done about that issue ought to demonstrate a clear grasp of the principle that "Christ died for our sins according to the Scriptures".

Thirdly, we should ask how a person's understanding of doctrine shows itself in their manner of life. The Prayer Book Ordinal urges priests to,

> ... endeavour yourselves from time to time to sanctify the lives of you and yours, and to fashion them after the rule and doctrine of Christ, that ye may be wholesome and godly examples and patterns for the people to follow.

Not that we should expect people to be perfect, but we should expect them to show a sharp awareness of the 'perfect pattern' that they are to follow. Once again, John Chapman gives a handy pointer when he says we should watch out for problems with "gold, grog and girls".

In the present climate, this means we must ask them detailed questions about their understanding of human sexuality, and specifically their views on same-sex relationships. One of our leading patronage bodies has found out the hard way they cannot assume that someone who declares themselves to be an evangelical will adopt a traditional biblical line on sexual matters. Whilst we undoubtedly need to work at deepening our understanding in this area, in the end we must be clear about, and insist on sticking to, the biblical pattern of sexuality that stems from seeing marriage as a reflection of what the *Book of Common Prayer* calls "the mystical union that is betwixt Christ and his Church".

The harsh truth is that we need constant vigilance to guard not

---

[80] 'Evangelism Explosion', devised by D James Kennedy, popularised the question, "If you were to die tonight, and God asked why he should let you into heaven, what would you reply?" The form of the question suggested here comes to the same thing, though it is arguably more 'theologically correct'.

only the gospel (cf 1 Tim 6:20), but those institutions which have been established to promote the gospel both nationally and within the Church of England. Ultimately, of course, it is the Church of England itself which ought to be "the pillar and foundation of the truth" (1 Tim 3:15), but we have a long way to go in achieving that. And this is all the more reason why we must be careful to preserve the gains made in Anglican institutions in the past.

No one should be appointed to a position of responsibility in an Anglican evangelical institution who will not uphold the core principles of Anglican evangelicalism. Theologically, we need not ask any more of them than this. But equally, we ought not to allow any less.

Contending together

As I have indicated throughout, both wings of contemporary Anglican evangelicalism are failing to transform the Church of England for the proclamation of the gospel. The conservative evangelicals are too negative in the stance they adopt towards the institution, the open evangelicals simply too positive.

The approach suggested here is neither automatically to *condemn* the institution through an attitude of suspicious cynicism, nor to *condone* it through a false optimism about Anglican comprehensiveness. Rather, we must *contend* for it.

This will be a challenge to conservative and open evangelicals alike. As we have argued from the outset, our aim must be nothing less than the transformation of the *whole* denomination. That was the understanding expressed in *Towards the Conversion of England*, and that should be our desire now. Yet whilst conservative evangelicals see this as either too ambitious or too slow (rejecting the idea as something that has been 'tried and failed', and preferring instead to 'get on with' ministry locally and to plant churches elsewhere), open evangelicals seem to regard the idea with suspicion — as if it is improper to want the Church of England to change its attitude on evangelism and conversion.

Yet the harsh reality is that the necessary changes in the national agenda will not come about without 'root and branch' change in the institutional structures, and that will not happen accidentally.

Conservative evangelicals need to accept it will not happen through the model of 'flagship churches' and unofficial church plants. Since the 1950s, they have rightly been proud of their 'big gun' congregations — All Souls Langham Place, St Helen's Bishopsgate, Christ Church Fullwood, Jesmond parish church Newcastle, and so on. But the fact that one can so easily name these congregations illustrates the problem — there are simply too few of them. Similarly, however many new churches are planted, they are not appearing at a sufficient rate either to transform the Church or, in the foreseeable future, to convert the nation.

Meanwhile, the vast majority of evangelical ministers are working in ordinary parishes with average-sized congregations, unsupported by the institutional structures and unacknowledged by the evangelical subculture, which saves its accolades for the 'big church' ministers.[81]

The open evangelicals, on the other hand, seem rather to hope that the institution may accept their point of view in the same way that they have accepted its own. Meanwhile, they are happy enough doing their thing, but there are no plans to challenge and change the 'thing' other people are doing — which is all part of the principle of being 'open' and 'accepting'.

That, of course, is all well and good, provided you can be sure that what others are doing is also proclaiming the gospel so that people may be converted. Yet, as we have pointed out, the *prima facie* evidence throughout the Church of England is that this is not, in fact, the case.

For conservative evangelicals, then, the challenge is to contend

---

[81] Some conservative evangelicals recently came up with a proposal to make the 'big church' leaders into local 'bishops', thereby reinforcing the view that it is the size of your congregation that really counts, not the effort put into your ministry (or even necessarily your ability to work with and lead other clergy).

for the Church of England. For open evangelicals, the challenge is *to contend* for the Church of England. In both cases, however, there will be a need to contend *alongside others*, and this means being willing both to lead and to be lead.

Unfortunately, leading evangelicals is like trying to herd cats. Once again, therefore, the first need is for a change in our own attitudes.

Above all, we need to get back to meeting together relationally and face-to-face as evangelicals committed to a cause. Fortunately, there is a structure already in place for this. Unfortunately, it has somewhat fallen into disuse.

In most of the dioceses throughout the Church of England, you will find a diocesan Evangelical Union or Fellowship. Not so long ago, these would have been the automatic starting point for any evangelical minister newly arrived in the diocese. These fellowships were open to clergy and laity, and most of them organized regular meetings where people would gather to be encouraged and to support one another. They also formed the electoral base for the Church of England Evangelical Council (CEEC), which aims to be the voice of evangelical Anglicanism.

The reasons why these fellowships have ceased to function effectively may be many, but as I indicated in Part 1, evangelical divisions have certainly had a part to play. Yet we cannot expect to contend for the national institution if we cannot get along together in our own dioceses. As a basic starting point, then, evangelicals ought to commit themselves to grass-roots involvement in the local evangelical fellowship.

Secondly, we need to agree to think *denominationally*, but we need to realize that the denomination is 'us' not 'them'. There may be more of 'them' than 'us', locally perhaps or even nationally, but that ought not to force us into ghettos or enclaves. Article XXVI recognizes that,

> ... in the visible Church the evil be ever mingled with the good, and
> sometime the evil have chief authority in the ministration of the word

and sacraments.

However, it does not regard this as an excuse either for giving up on the institution or for ignoring the problem.

Here, the 'big church' leaders have a special rôle to play, because they have significant clout to exercise. As at June 2005, the majority of the 172 larger churches in the Church of England (those having over 350 members) were evangelical, and they represented an astonishing *quarter* of all the evangelicals in the Anglican Church.[82] Often such churches are major financial contributors to the diocese, and they may be sending significant numbers of people into full-time ministry.

Yet few, if any, of these large churches exercise a *denominational* strategy. On the contrary, the impression is that they keep themselves very much apart from the institution, and indeed may attribute their success to this separation.

The one major exception is Holy Trinity Brompton, which has brilliantly exploited its national and international influence and its relationship with the institutional Church, to the extent that it has not only been able to plant congregations in 'failing' situations in England, but it effectively has its own theological college, responsible for training clergy from two of the largest dioceses — London and Chelmsford.[83]

Personally, I have serious difficulties with the theological stance of HTB, but they have undoubtedly shown the way in terms of engagement with the structures.[84] Why should other churches not follow where they have led? The answer must surely be that it is not regarded as being a right, or perhaps even a *proper*, strategy. Yet it

---

[82] See 'Large Anglican Churches: some facts and figures from Christian Research', http://www.e-n.org.uk/p-3246-Large-Anglican-churches.htm, retrieved 23 August 2011.

[83] St Mellitus College.

[84] Indeed, I would go as far as to say that HTB has occasionally shown serious lapses of theological judgement, including being the springboard for the 'Toronto Blessing' in this country and giving a teaching platform to 'open theists' — quite apart from the 'two stage blessing' approach of the Alpha Course itself. Nevertheless, their positive approach to the institution has undoubtedly worked.

has clearly been effective!

There is an urgent need amongst evangelicals for a generation of leaders who will take up their national, *denominational*, leadership rôles, and in this the big churches could make a significant impact and set a powerful example.

Thirdly, we need to agree to *be lead*, which means agreeing to act together. Here again, diocesan evangelical fellowships can help by bringing people together. However, when we come together we need to act 'politically' in the broad sense of the word, meaning with regard to how the institution of the Church is organized and governs its collective life.

Indeed, it is arguably the absence of such action which has contributed to the moribund nature of our these fellowships. It is all very well meeting up with our evangelical friends for a coffee and chat and a chance to listen to an interesting speaker. For some clergy, this provides a welcome escape from the frantic pace of parish life. Yet is this worth giving up an evening or a Saturday morning, especially when more congenial fellowship is to be found in less diverse groups?

The answer to such objections, however, is to shift the focus away from 'me and my needs' to the Church and society's needs. Coming to the evangelical fellowship for what I can get out of it is like going to Sunday church for what I can get out of that. Certainly I have my needs, but the basis and aim of both gatherings should surely be what we find in Hebrews 10:23-25,

> Let us hold unswervingly to the hope we profess, for he who promised is faithful. And let us consider how we may spur one another on toward love and good deeds. Let us not give up meeting together, as some are in the habit of doing, but let us encourage one another — and all the more as you see the Day approaching.

We should gather specifically as evangelicals because the whole Church of England is not (yet) committed to the task of evangelism. We gather, furthermore, because we ourselves need encouragement not to swerve from the hope we possess (unless we think we are of sterner stuff than the recipients of Hebrews), to spur one another on as we see the approaching Day of judgement and because there are people in non-evangelizing parishes who need to hear the gospel.

Yet while there are loud voices today calling for a 'wider representation' on the CEEC of the different 'strands' of evangelicalism, the fact is that those strands can't even get together at a local level, so fundamental is the sense of distrust in some cases. Meanwhile, diocesan structures continue untroubled and often without any real commitment to an evangelistic agenda.

Case study: the vicissitudes of a diocesan evangelical fellowship

In the early 1980s, the Chelmsford Diocesan Evangelical Association was typical of many such fellowships across the country. Meetings were well attended by clergy and laity and all the diocesan 'stalwarts' would be there. The CDEA also published a regular newsletter with information about individuals and parishes. There was a general sense that we all 'knew what we were about' and an expectation that membership of the CDEA was a normal part of being evangelical.

All that changed with the changing face of evangelicalism. As our unity diminished, so did membership of the CDEA. Gradually the organizing committee became more conservative, which led to a general withdrawal of more senior open evangelical clergy. Eventually, the CDEA was 'mothballed' as no longer providing a useful meeting point for a fragmented constituency.

Three years ago, however, the CDEA was relaunched. The initiative came from the conservative wing, but the intention was to involve as many as possible from the wider evangelical spectrum. After a promising start, the CDEA has struggled to make headway and it is noticeable that open evangelical affiliation is still very tenuous. Nevertheless, the committee has been broadened and perseveres in trying to recreate an effective local evangelical body.

In all this, there is a particular rôle for the laity. The Church of England is governed through a series of synods — deanery, diocesan and general (national) — and administered through numerous diocesan boards and committees. A large percentage of the members of these bodies are lay people. Most of them are dedicated and sincere, but very few of them come from evangelical churches or have an 'evangelizing' attitude.

A serious-minded evangelical body within a diocese ought surely to make every effort to ensure that as many as possible of these diocesan posts are filled with clear-thinking, passionate evangelicals with a vision for the proclamation of the gospel and the transformation of the Church.

The problem, so often, is that this is not encouraged collectively, and so the few individuals who put themselves forward are often isolated and unsupported by their local churches. If we are not to feed people piecemeal into the institutional structures, where they eventually become discouraged and exhausted, we must have an explicit and mutually-understood strategy of involvement in diocesan life, not only in the local congregation but in the wider evangelical constituency.

An explicit element of the programme of diocesan evangelical fellowships and unions therefore ought to be the encouragement of lay, as well as clerical, involvement in diocesan life, especially where it involves *policy making*. This does not exclude less-glamorous things like the parsonages board (which looks after clergy housing — but remember the seven in Acts 6) and would certainly include the Diocesan Advisory Committee, which does more than advise but actually intervenes on matters like the redesign of church-building interiors. It would also include boards of mission, education and so on.

We must also not forget the vacancy-in-see committee — an oddly-Anglican 'Cinderella' institution which does nothing most of the time until a bishop retires or dies (both of which can happen at short notice), when suddenly it is crucial to the appointment of the next bishop of the diocese (the 'see' which has now become 'vacant'). Evangelicals should always aim to have members on this body.

To take such a deliberate approach to diocesan 'politics' (which, we must remember, means simply the way the *'polis'* or community is governed) would require a transformation of evangelical attitudes, but it would surely be worth it for the 'conversion of England' — or at least that part of it represented by the local diocese.

ERIC and the transformation of the Church

The first section of *Towards the Conversion of England* was headed 'The Situation Facing the Church', and that situation is certainly no better today than it was then. Indeed, as the outbreak of chaos and looting showed in the late summer of 2011, England is increasingly experiencing the overt effects of its 'de-Christianization'.

The authors of the report lamented indicators of 'moral decline' that most today would find laughable.[85] Yet the fact that we find their attitude amusing is a reflection on us as much as on them. The social and medical problems of alcohol have vastly increased since the 1950s, sexually transmitted diseases are held in check only by improved medical treatments, 'illegitimacy' is almost the norm and

---

[85] "The war has revealed, and also accelerated, a sharp decline in truthfulness and personal honesty, and an alarming spread of sexual laxity, and of the gambling fever. [...] Magistrates have expressed their anxiety at the rise (in the serious nature as well as in the quantity) of juvenile crime. School teachers complain of the difficulty of impressing upon their young charges the abomination of lying and stealing which they copy from their elders at home. The Government has found it necessary to resort to poster propaganda against venereal disease, and to issue to all medical officers of health a circular on the problem of illegitimate babies. In the past 30 years the number of divorces has risen from upwards of 500 a year to approximately 12,250 in 1944." (*Towards the Conversion of England*, paragraph 7).

personal debt cripples the lives of those who are already materially poor.

This is not the time for you doing your thing in your small corner of the Lord's vineyard and I doing my thing in mine, whilst the bulk of the Church of England drifts on with its deliberate embracing of theological ambiguity. Before we can act, however, we need to be clear about what we are trying to achieve. According to the principles established in *Towards the Conversion of England*, our twin aims should be (a) to seek people's conversion through the proclamation of the gospel, and (b) to the seek the transformation of the Church for gospel proclamation.

Evangelicals, who are already committed to the first aim should be encouraging and engaging in evangelism as and when they can — in season and out of season. But they should also be deliberately seeking to change the institution so that it increasingly becomes 'evangelistic' in its attitude and actions.

Our efforts must therefore go in two directions at once: ministering to those who need to hear the gospel and contending within the Church so as to bring the institution round to the shared task of gospel proclamation.

All this needs to be clearly understood by ourselves and explicitly presented to others, and in this regard the acronym ERIC may help: Explain, Recruit, Initiate, Coordinate.

EXPLAIN: We need to explain to other people what we are doing and why we are doing it. This is not just a matter of telling them what we are about (though it includes that). It means getting them to see and share the vision of a transformed Church seeking to honour the Saviour by proclaiming the gospel.

RECRUIT: We need to recruit people to involvement in this project. This means getting them not just to share the vision of a transformed Church but to see the importance of evangelizing a nation of lost people.

INITIATE: We need to initiate, developing new projects for evangelistic ministry and finding ways in which we can further the transformation of the Church using what lies to hand locally.

COORDINATE: We need to coordinate, sharing what is happening with others locally and across the country and hearing from them, so that we do not become isolated and discouraged, or complacent when things may be going well in our area. So-called social media can help with this as can the internet more generally. Thus, for example, the AEJCC has a 'Facebook' page. Others may find other ways of providing this coordination.

If you have read and generally agreed with this book so far, could I urge you to take on these principles yourself, and become one of those who explains, recruits, initiates and coordinates with others in the transformation of the Church of England where you are? Don't wait for someone else either to take the lead or give the permission. If you have the vision, that is what it takes, and if you have the desire, there are others willing to help.

The mission of the church and the *missio dei*

Missionary work must be either the relation of the Church to the world, or a fad of a few.[86]

For many evangelicals, much of what has been said will have made uncomfortable reading. Some will regard the idea of working for the transformation of the Church as a lost cause. "It will take too long," they argue, "and in any case the difficulties are too great. Let us get on with preaching the gospel as we can and planting new churches where we may."

For others, the idea of transforming the Church smacks of arrogance, of the idea that evangelicals have 'got it right' or 'know it all', when there are clearly many things we have got wrong and do not know. To them, this is all rather un-Anglican and even un-Christian. The Church of England contains many traditions, each with its own emphases. Accepting this is of the essence of what it means to be an Anglican.

---

[86] Roland Allen, *The Spontaneous Expansion of the Church*, chapter 7, 'Missionary Organization'.

In response, I would say that both these attitudes actually display a defective ecclesiology — a misunderstanding of the Church.

Evangelicals have often been accused of this, but the accusers themselves have, I suggest, also had a defective ecclesiology, ironically in just the same way as those whom they accuse.[87]

The real defect on the part of both those who stand somewhat aloof from the Church and those who embrace it is not in a *structural* understanding of what constitutes the Church by way of its membership, its ministries, its services or its organization. It is not even in failing to see that God calls us to be members of the Church, rather than just individual believers in Jesus (though that mistake is certainly made).

Rather, the defect is in our *functional* understanding, in failing to see what the Church is actually *for*. At the heart of this lies a fundamental question about God's action in the world.

In *A Guide to the Church of England*, Martin Davie refers to the much-used concept of the *missio dei*.[88] This is actually a Latin expression which can be translated simply as 'the mission of God'. So why use the Latin? Davie again quotes Paul Avis:

> The Latin term is necessary because it holds a depth and power that English translations [*sic* plural] cannot capture: the mission of God, the mission that belongs to God, the mission that flows from the heart of God. *Missio dei* speaks of the overflowing of God's being and nature into God's purposeful activity in the world.[89]

Personally, I am inclined to think this use of Latin may be more like those menus that put everything in French to make it look good. When the food arrives, however, your *pommes frites* are still just chips. Moreover, given that Latin is *not* the original language of the biblical revelation, there is surely a danger in insisting on the

---

[87] Archbishop Robert Runcie, a definite Liberal-Catholic in his churchmanship, famously made this accusation at the third, Caister, NEAC — and was applauded by the audience at the end of his speech!

[88] Martin Davie, *A guide to the Church of England* (London: Mowbray, 2008), 202-207.

[89] *Ibid.* 202.

nuances of Latin that we are saying something that is not in the Bible.[90]

The use of Latin may give the idea of God's mission a certain 'aura', but it may also mislead our own thinking about the Church's rôle. Thus Davie concludes (correctly),

> Saying that the mission of the Church is rooted in the *missio dei* thus means saying that the Church's mission does not begin with the activity of human beings but the activity of God himself.[91]

But then Davie adds, "The mission of the Church is its participation in this activity."[92] And he quotes from a joint Anglican-Methodist document:

> By the power of the Holy Spirit, God graciously enables us, as unworthy but forgiven sinners, to participate in the mission of God. [...] 'The Church's task is to participate in God's mission' [...].[93]

Unfortunately, there are two ways this 'participation' can be understood. Properly speaking, it means that God's mission to the world flows *from* Christ *through* the Church, and thence back to God as all things are reconciled to him. This is surely the pattern we find in 2 Corinthians 5:18-20:

> All this is from God, who reconciled us to himself through Christ and gave us the ministry of reconciliation: that God was reconciling the world to himself in Christ, not counting men's sins against them. And he has committed to us the message of reconciliation. We are therefore Christ's ambassadors, as though God were making his appeal through us. We implore you on Christ's behalf: Be reconciled to God.

Unfortunately, the language of 'participation' is sometimes used in such a way that the Church is sidelined — as if it is an adjunct to

---

[90] In this context, Alister McGrath's *Iustitia Dei: A History of the Christian Doctrine of Justification* (Cambridge: Cambridge University Press, 1989) gives an appropriately cautionary tale of how the Vulgate Latin translation of the biblical words for 'righteousness' and 'justification' threw Western theology off-course for centuries (see pp 4-16).

[91] Martin Davie, *A guide to the Church of England* (London: Mowbray, 2008), 202.

[92] *Ibid.*

[93] *Ibid.* 202-203.

God's mission, rather than the primary *means* to that mission. According to this view, God is doing something profound in the world — carrying on the *missio dei* — and we have to try to work out what it is (rather like a developing Rolf Harris sketch) and join in where we can. And this creates the further danger that the Church can be perceived to exist *without* being involved in mission.

As the introductory quote from Roland Allen suggests, however, if the Church does not relate to the world first and foremost as God's mission agent then 'missionary' activity becomes a 'fad' — something done by those who are enthusiastic about that sort of thing. In fact you get precisely what we observe in the Church of England today. There are 'evangelicals', keen on evangelism, and there are others (actually the majority) for whom evangelism is a somewhat uncomfortable concept, something best left to others — the vicar, perhaps, or even to other churches.[94]

Yet evangelicals themselves fall into exactly the same trap when they set up 'mission societies', for what this says in effect is that the Church is *not* a mission society but something else and that mission therefore requires new structures.

It is this which is the truly defective ecclesiology — the notion that there is the Church *and* there is mission — that, and the idea which we looked at earlier that evangelism is *part* of mission rather than the *heart* of mission.

The great missionary to Muslims, Jens Christensen, made the same point. So often, he observed, Christians look for a 'means' by which they can carry out mission. Christensen says in response,

> The Church is the creation of God, to be used by Him to proclaim His message. In other words, the Church is God's *means*.[95]

Yet typically, evangelical Anglicans of every stripe have looked for a 'means' to evangelize other than the Church itself.

---

[94] The Bishop of Chelmsford, Stephen Cottrell, has been encouraging deaneries to run missions which must, in his words, be "evangelistic". In my own deanery, however, a discussion about what exactly *is* evangelism got quite bogged down.

[95] Jens Christensen, *Mission to Islam and Beyond*, (Blackwood South Australia: New Creations Publications, 2001), 15.

Evangelicals who cannot be *bothered* with the transformation of the Church imagine they can 'preach the gospel' *despite* the Church. They believe they can, as it were, make themselves heard above the noise of meaningless static coming from within the wider Church. In this case, *the Church* is seen as *additional* to evangelistic proclamation. And according to this view, the gospel can be proclaimed by *other means* than the Church.

Historically, this has manifested itself the establishment of missionary bodies. Recently, it results in 'church plants' which will be labelled as Anglican, but which will do something not being done by the existing Anglican church in the parish.

On the other hand, evangelicals who see no need to transform the Church into an instrument for gospel proclamation believe that the Church can still be true to its calling whether or not it is aiming at the conversion of others. In this case, *evangelistic proclamation* is additional to *the Church*, which is regarded in practice as if it can still be 'the Church' even when it is not specifically proclaiming the gospel.

This manifests itself in a refusal to criticize what happens in these other churches, coupled with a fierce antagonism to the 'church planters'.

Yet properly speaking, the Church *is* the missionary organization seeking people's conversion, or if it is not the missionary organization it is not the Church.

The next step

One of the popular 'definitions' of madness is to keep doing the same thing whilst expecting a different result, and Anglican evangelicals have been doing the same thing for over a century, since the rise of 'ritualism'.

This 'thing' consists of a cycle of expansion, confrontation, division, recrimination, dissipation and regeneration.[96]

---

[96] This is ably, if somewhat depressingly, illustrated in James Whisenant's, *A Fragile Unity: Anti-ritualism and the Division of Anglican Evangelicalism in the Nineteenth Century* (Milton Keynes: Paternoster Press, 2004).

The 'expansion' phase is the outcome of evangelism itself. Evangelicals tend to grow in numbers because they evangelize. Even today, with most Anglican congregations still in decline, evangelical congregations are shrinking more slowly than the rest, and therefore proportionally their numbers are increasing.[97] Nevertheless, they are still a minority.

When they reach a certain critical mass, however, evangelicals are in a position for 'confrontation' with what is happening in the institution. In this century, the 1967 Keele NEAC represents just such a point, when it really began to matter whether evangelicals collectively stayed in the Church of England or not. In the nineteenth century, the confrontation took the form of pamphleteering and legal action with regard to ritualism.

At this point, 'division' occurs over tactics. Some evangelicals want to be very confrontational, others more eirenical, towards those with whom they disagree, who nevertheless make up a significant proportion of the institution. Accusations of compromise or inflexibility fly backwards and forwards and we enter the 'recrimination' phase. This happened in the latter period of the ritualist controversy and again in the 1980s.

As evangelicals separate into their own 'parties', so we enter the 'dissipation' phase. Without their unity, they can no longer 'confront' the institutional issues in sufficient numbers. Moreover, some of those who advocated a more low-key approach will indeed wind up compromising. Others will accept the institutional *status quo*, still others will withdraw from the institutional structures entirely. Erstwhile friends become estranged and relationships strained. We are clearly in just such a phase now.[98]

---

[97] 'Large Anglican Churches: some facts and figures from Christian Research', *op. cit.*

[98] It is interesting to look at the later careers of some of those who contributed to the 1995 publication, *Has Keele Failed?* By no means all have continued their association with their earlier evangelicalism.

Finally, however, comes a period of regeneration. The old battles are forgotten and the old warriors retire. A new generation of evangelicals emerge who focus, once again, on evangelism. So the number of evangelicals begins to increase and a new cycle is ready to begin. But the new generation know little or nothing of the past and therefore history is destined to repeat itself. This happened in post-war England and, unless we actually learn our lessons, it is bound to happen again at some time in the future.

Much of what is being advocated here by way of strategy has actually been suggested before, in the 'division' phase of the conflict with nineteenth century ritualism and again in the 'Keele' generation.[99] "If only we will play our part in the institution," the suggestion goes, "all will be well." But it wasn't then, so why should things be any different this time round?

The answer is that we must shift our primary goal away from either seeking to preserve the institution from others or seeking to make it more comfortable for ourselves. Instead, we must look to the Church's true task: to seek people's conversion through the proclamation of the gospel. And in the light of this we must seek the transformation of the Church for gospel proclamation.

Since the publication of *Towards the Conversion of England,* the Church has had sixty-six years of *not* doing just that. We cannot allow another sixty-six to pass. Evangelicals, of all people, should have a vision for something different, but we ourselves must change before this will happen.

> FOR IT IS TIME FOR JUDGEMENT TO BEGIN WITH THE FAMILY OF GOD... (1 PETER 4:17)

---

[99] See Whisenant, *op cit.*

Bibliography and other reading

Advisory Council for the Church's Ministry and Tiller, John, *A Strategy for the Church's Ministry* (London: Church Information Office, 1983)

The Archbishops' Council of the Church of England, *Working with the Spirit: choosing diocesan bishops — a review of the operation of the Crown Appointments Commission and related matters* (London: Church House Publishing, 2001)

Allen, Roland, *The Spontaneous Expansion of the Church* (Grand Rapids: W B Eerdmans Publishing Company, 1962)

Atherstone, Andrew, *An Anglican Evangelical Identity Crisis : The Churchman-Anvil Affair of 1981-1984* (London: Latimer Trust, 2008)

Avis, Paul, *The Anglican Understanding of the Church: An Introduction* (London: SPCK, 2000)

Barclay, Oliver, *Evangelicalism in Britain 1935-1995: A Personal Sketch* (Leicester: Inter-Varsity Press, 1997)

Bolt, Peter, *Mission Minded: A Tool for Planning your Ministry around Christ's Mission* (Kingsford NSW: St Matthias Press, 1992)

Bray, Gerald L, *Documents of the English Reformation* (Cambridge: James Clarke & Co Ltd)2004

Brown, Callum G, *The Death of Christian Britain* (Routledge, 2000)

Buchanan, Colin, *What did Cranmer think he was doing?* (Bramcote: Grove Books, 1976)

Buchanan, Colin, *Cut the Connection: Disestablishment and the Church of England* (London: Darton Longman & Todd, 1994)

Buchanan, Colin, *Is the Church of England Biblical?: An Anglican Ecclesiology* (London: Darton Longman & Todd, 1998)

Christensen, Jens, *Mission to Islam and Beyond*, (Blackwood South Australia: New Creations Publications, 2001), available at www.answering-islam.org/Books/Christensen/christen sen.pdf

Church of England, *The Mystery of Salvation – A report by the Doctrine Commission of the Church of England*, (London: Church House Publishing, 1995)

Collinson, Patrick, *The Elizabethan Puritan Movement*, (London: Jonathan Cape, 1967)

Commission on Evangelism, *Towards the Conversion of England* (London: The Press and Publications Board of the Church Assembly, 1945)

Davie, Martin, *A guide to the Church of England* (London: Mowbray, 2008)

Eddison, John, *A Study in Spiritual Power: An Appreciation of E J H Nash (Bash)* (Crowborough: Highland Books, 1992)

Executive Committee of the Second National Evangelical Anglican Congress, *The Nottingham Statement* (London: Church Pastoral Aid Society, 1977)

Finke, Roger, and Stark, Rodney, *The Churching of America, 1776-1990* (Rutgers University Press, 1999)

Gill, Robin, *The Myth of the Empty Church* (London: SPCK, 1993)

Gill, Robin, *Strategic Church Leadership* (London: SPCK, 1996)

Gill, Robin, *The Empty Church Revisited* (Ashgate Publishing Limited, 2003)

Jackson, Bob, *Hope for the Church: Contemporary Strategies for Growth* (London: Church House, 2002)

Jackson, Bob, *The Road to Growth: Towards a Thriving Church* (London: Church House, 2005)

Judd, Stephen & Cable, Kenneth, *Sydney Anglicans: A History of the Diocese* (Sydney: Anglican Information Office, 1987)

McGrath, Alister, *Iustitia Dei: A History of the Christian Doctrine of Justification* (Cambridge: Cambridge University Press, 1989)

Murray, Iain H, *Evangelicalism Divided: A Record of Crucial Change in the Years 1950 to 2000* (The Banner of Truth Trust, 2000)

Mwaluda, Samson, *Reorienting a Church for Accelerated Growth: With Special Reference to the Anglican Diocese of Taita Taveta, Kenya* (Nairobi: Uzima, 2003)

Neill, Stephen, *Anglicanism* (Harmondsworth: Penguin, 1965)

Orpwood, Michael, *Chappo: For the Sake of the Gospel — John Chapman and the Department of Evangelism* (Russell Lea: Eagleswift Press, 1995)

Packer, James, *Evangelism and the Sovereignty of God* (Leicester: Inter-Varsity Press, 1976)

Reed, John, *Glorious Battle: The Cultural Politics of Victorian Anglo-Catholicism* (London: Tufton Books, 1998)

Robinson, John A T, *Honest to God* (London: SCM Press, 1963)

Turnbull, Richard, *Anglican and Evangelical?: Can They Agree?* (London: Continuum International Publishing Group Ltd., 2007)

Whisenant, James C, *A Fragile Unity: Anti-ritualism and the Division of Anglican Evangelicalism in the Nineteenth Century* (Milton Keynes: Paternoster Press, 2004)

Wright, Tom, *Surprised by Hope* (London: SPCK, 2007)

Yeats, Charles, *Has Keele Failed?: Reform in the Church of England* (London: Hodder & Stoughton, 1995)

Index